PHOTOGRAPHY BY
Jason Lowe

A *year in my kitchen*

SKYE
GYNGELL

QUADRILLE

First published in 2006 by
Quadrille Publishing Limited
Alhambra House
27-31 Charing Cross Road
London WC2H 0LS
www.quadrille.co.uk

Text © 2006 Skye Gyngell

Photography © 2006 Jason Lowe

Design and layout © 2006 Quadrille
Publishing Limited

Hardback edition first published in 2006
Reprinted in 2007 (three times)
10 9 8 7 6 5 4

Paperback edition first published in 2007
10 9 8 7 6 5 4 3 2 1

Cataloguing in Publication Data:
a catalogue record for this book is available
from the British Library.

ISBN: 978 184400 337 2 (Hardback)

ISBN: 978 184400 5925 (Paperback)

Printed in China

Publishing director Jane O'Shea
Creative director Helen Lewis
Project editor Janet Illsley
Art direction & design
Lawrence Morton
Photographer Jason Lowe
Stylist Cynthia Inions
Production Bridget Fish

notes

Please use sea salt, freshly ground pepper
and fresh herbs (except in the rare instances
where I have specified dried herbs).

I use medium eggs – organic and free-range.
Anyone who is pregnant or in a vulnerable
health group should avoid recipes using raw
egg whites or lightly cooked eggs.

Timings are for fan-assisted ovens. If using a
conventional oven, increase the temperature
by 10–15°C (1/2 Gas mark). Use an oven
thermometer to check the temperature.

Introduction

Fresh, ripe, seasonal ingredients are at the core of my
cooking. There is a wonderful sense of anticipation,
as well as a comforting familiarity, if you cook with the
seasons. For instance, knowing that sweet, juicy damsons
will be here for their short two-week stay around mid-
September, or that the complex flavour of blood oranges
will bring a warm glow to the barren winter months of
January and February is deeply reassuring.

It is June as I write and the first cherries are making their
short appearance – bringing with them happy childhood
memories. Come autumn, Kentish cobnuts will be available
and beautiful walnuts arrive from Périgord. Cooking with
the seasons provides a sense of life's continuity – a feeling
that everything is just right with the world... an ease with
ingredients naturally follows.

At the nursery, we source ingredients as locally as possible and I urge you to do the same. Seek out quality suppliers, ideally supporting your local greengrocer, fishmonger, butcher and/or farmers' market. It is a good way to learn more about the food you are eating and helps you to make a connection with the earth, seasons, environment and the people around you. I find it impossible to make that connection through supermarket shopping alone.

Good food begins with good ingredients, carefully sourced and at their seasonal best, but what really makes a good cook? Certainly, it has to do with practice and accumulated experience. As with any skill, the more frequently it is performed, the more confidence and knowledge will be gained. It is also important to begin to understand the rationale behind certain techniques – to appreciate what you are doing and why.

However, it is perhaps even more crucial to develop a feel and intuition for food and cooking. Then heart, hands and head work together to produce something worthwhile.

A recipe is simply a documentation of a cooking process. Its function is to provide a list of ingredients and an idea of the method and structure of a dish, which is invaluable to the inexperienced cook. But merely following a recipe is ultimately an unfulfilling experience, unless you learn to apply all your senses – taste and sight of course, but also smell, touch and emotion. Only then will you begin to understand the very nature of the dish.

Ask yourself questions about produce before you buy: "Where does it come from?", "Is it fresh?", "In season?", "Grown locally?", "Does it really inspire me to cook?", "Does its very appearance make me hungry?".

Tasting food as you cook is very important. To rest assured that a dish will be fine because you have followed a recipe is an incorrect assumption. Taste, pause and consider what the dish needs. More often than not, it will be attention to seasoning, or perhaps a little lemon zest or finely chopped parsley to clean up the flavours... or possibly nothing at all!

I don't see food as a work of art. Certainly, thought and composition are important. Food on a plate should appeal to the eye as well as the palate, but never at the expense of flavour. When clever technique and fragile structures are all that are considered, a dish will live only for a short time in the memory.

My greatest learning experience in the last few years has been working with a kitchen garden. At Petersham, our garden is modest, but it has provided me with a direct and immediate appreciation of the seasons, as well as an awe-inspiring respect for the richness of the earth. I have learnt to feel a deep respect for the abundance that nature provides.

For me, to cook is the most natural thing in the world. To work professionally as a chef can be very demanding, exhausting and incredibly stressful – probably one of the least glamorous jobs for a woman! Yet I love it today as much as when I first started and I still dream about food when I sleep! I can't think of anything more exciting than to welcome in the new season's ingredients.

Above all, for me, cooking is an act of love and giving. It is about breaking bread with family and friends, about conviviality and shared experience. As you glance through this book, I wish that you may begin to feel a little of the joy and deep sense of fulfilment that cooking has brought to my life. I sincerely hope that if you've not yet experienced the joy of cooking, it is waiting for you just around the corner.

Happy cooking!

Food only ever really sings if you have put your heart and soul into it. Taste as you go along and feel free to put your own stamp on a dish – I cook what I feel is right.

A love of eating and a real appreciation of great produce – combined with a generosity of spirit and the desire to share with others – is at the core of beautiful food.

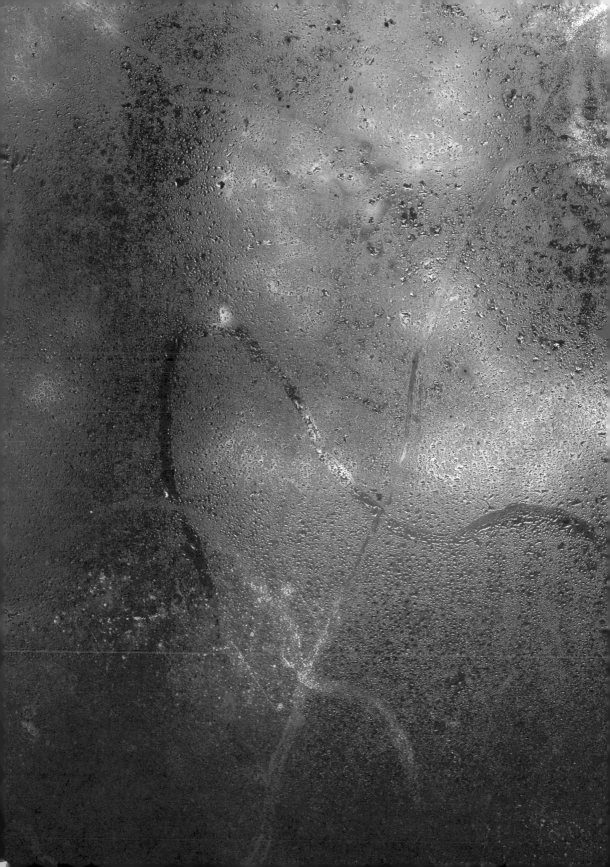

MY TOOLBOX

The toolbox is the 'nuts and bolts' of my cooking. As the seasons change and new ingredients present themselves, it is the toolbox I turn to for inspiration. Over the years, I have found that these tools enable me to bring out the full natural flavours of seasonal ingredients and inspire me to create new dishes.

Every item in the toolbox works as a component to be added to something else – the 'tools' act as conductors or enhancers of flavour and they come alive when they are added to another dish. They work without masking or overpowering the ingredients that I most want to highlight in a dish. Ultimately, they help me to achieve the balancing of flavours that is so critical to the way I cook. This toolbox really works for me and I hope it will for you too!

SKY

top note herbs

lemon zest

infused oils*

basil oil

vinaigrettes

mayonnaise bases

flavoured yoghurts

agra-dolce

roasted red onions

slow-roasted tomatoes

toasted nuts

sourdough breadcrumbs

braised lentils

tea-smoking

stock

roasted spice mix

base note herbs

EARTH

Base notes & top notes

In every dish that I cook, I am looking for the purest possible taste – an entirety. I think of it like the notes of the scale – beginning with the earthy base note flavours and finishing with the top notes that add freshness and make the dish 'sing'.
In the way that I cook I am constantly seeking harmony – a balance of sweet, sour and salty tastes. This isn't a new concept, it is the way people have cooked in the East forever.

* chilli, garlic, lemon-infused

Base note herbs

I cannot imagine cooking without herbs, as I find them so essential to the taste of food. Base note herbs are the ones that help lay the foundations of a dish. They include bay, thyme, rosemary, sage, summer savory and lovage. Parsley, when added to bay and thyme, forms the trinity that we call a bouquet garni, which is an essential part of soups, stocks and slow-cooked dishes. Base note herbs endure the burden of long, slow cooking incredibly well, continuing to add their flavour as long as they are cooking.

Fresh herbs in season lend dishes an exceptional vibrancy and freshness. I really think that dried herbs (possibly with the exception of mint) are not worth using – they only contribute a musty staleness to a dish.

Roasted spice mix

I use this combination of spices a great deal, because their flavours work particularly well together, lending a depth and sensory aroma to many purées and slow-cooked dishes. They definitely belong at the earth end of the scale and must be used in conjunction with other flavours in order to balance and pad them out. The spice mix is a foundation that only really works if the heat of chilli is added, plus the sweetness of palm sugar or maple syrup, and the sourness of tamarind, lemon or lime. The saltiness of soy or fish sauce is also needed to underpin the spice mix flavour.

Buy whole spices for this – ready-ground spices will already have lost their freshness and give dishes a dull, musty taste. And for optimum flavour, use a pestle and mortar or spice grinder rather than a food processor to grind the mix. You can keep the roasted spice mix in a sealed container up to a month, but no longer.

for the roasted spice mix

1–2 cinnamon sticks
50g coriander seeds
50g cumin seeds
50g fennel seeds
50g mustard seeds
50g fenugreek seeds
5 cardamom pods
2–3 star anise (or cloves)

Place a dry, heavy-based frying pan (preferably non-stick) over a low heat. Break the cinnamon stick in half. Once a clear smoke begins to rise from your pan, add all the spices and cook, stirring frequently, to toast them. Be careful not to burn them though, as this would give a bitter taste. Once the seeds begin to pop, they are ready. Remove from the heat and grind to a fine powder. Store in an airtight container until ready to use.

Stock

The making of a good stock is an important foundation in cookery and one of the first things you learn as a young chef. In my mind, a stock cube is not a viable substitute – its flavour is essentially artificial and unpalatable when the stock is reduced down.

I have seen all sorts of things thrown into stocks as they are made – even red peppers, garlic and vegetable peelings. I am totally against these additions. Because a stock acts as a building block, it needs to have a very pure base flavour. Other flavours only cloud and confuse the taste. Another rule when making a stock is to avoid adding salt. This is in order that the stock can be reduced without it becoming too salty.

I use chicken stock for a wide range of dishes, but you can adapt this recipe if veal, beef or lamb stock is more appropriate to the dish, simply by substituting the bones. Veal bones, in particular, make a lovely stock.

for the chicken stock

2kg chicken bones
3 yellow onions, peeled
6 carrots, peeled
3 celery sticks
a little olive oil
20 black peppercorns
4 bay leaves
small bunch of thyme
bunch of curly or flat leaf parsley
4 litres water

Preheat the oven to 200°C/Gas 6. Lay the chicken bones in a large baking tray and roast on the top shelf of the oven for about 15 minutes until golden brown. Meanwhile, roughly chop the onions, carrots and celery and place in a large stockpot or saucepan. Add the tiniest amount of olive oil and sweat over a low heat until the vegetables soften slightly and start to release their flavours.

When the bones are nicely coloured, add them to the vegetables along with black peppercorns, bay leaves, thyme and parsley. Pour in the water and bring just to the boil. Immediately, turn the heat down to low and cook gently for 1¹/2 hours, skimming the scum from the surface every now and then. It is very important that a stock does not boil, as this causes the impurities to be dragged back down into the stock rather than collect on the surface where they can be removed.

At the end of the cooking time, you should have a pure, clean tasting stock. Remove from the heat and strain through a fine sieve. Use as required. If preparing ahead, cool and refrigerate for up to 3 days, or freeze until needed.

Tea-smoking

I first came across this way of infusing flavour into food in Australia. The technique is best applied to oily fish, such as trout, wild salmon or mackerel; it also works well with quail and chicken. You can experiment with any type of tea you like. I use Lapsang and Earl Grey because they both have a very fragrant quality, which imparts a delicate, aromatic flavour to the fish or meat.

You will also need a large sturdy baking tin with a tight-fitting lid, a wire cake cooling rack that will fit comfortably inside the baking tin and 4 small metal pudding basins to hold the wire rack in place. A good extractor fan is also handy as the smoking itself can impart a strong aroma... albeit delicious!

for the tea-smoking mixture

45g muscovado sugar
60g caster sugar
125g tea leaves

Shape 2 small cups from sturdy foil, 7–8cm across the top and 2–3cm deep. Mix the sugars and tea leaves in a bowl, then tip half this dry mixture into each foil cup and stand them in the baking tin, towards the middle. Position the 4 pudding bowls in the corners of the tin and balance the wire rack on top.

Now cut parchment paper in the shape of the food you are tea-smoking. Lay the paper on the wire rack and place the food on top. Turn on your extractor fan. Place the baking tin with the lid on top over a medium-high heat (you will most likely need to place it across two burners).

It will take about 10 minutes for the smoke to get going and start to flavour the food. The cooking time depends on what you are smoking and whether you are cooking it completely or only partially. Refer to specific recipes for cooking times.

Braised lentils

I rarely choose to combine protein with carbs, for me the mix is usually too heavy. However, I do like to work with pulses, especially lentils. Scattered over a dish, their earthy flavour and texture lend a real depth without detracting or masking the flavours of the other ingredients. The little brown Castelluccio lentils from Umbria in Italy are my favourite. Puy lentils are also very good and may be easier for you to find. You need to be careful not to overcook lentils or they will become sludgy – they need to retain a definite bite.

for the lentils

500g Castelluccio or Puy lentils

1 red or yellow onion, peeled and quartered

1 carrot, peeled and cut into 3 chunks

1 red chilli

2 garlic cloves, peeled

2–3cm piece fresh root ginger, peeled and roughly chopped

5 thyme or parsley sprigs

2 bay leaves

1 tbsp chopped coriander root

2 tbsp sherry vinegar

2 tbsp tamari or soy sauce

2 tbsp sesame or walnut oil

Rinse the lentils and place them in a deep saucepan along with the onion, carrot, chilli, garlic cloves, ginger, thyme or parsley, bay leaves and coriander root. Add enough water to cover the lentils completely and bring to the boil over a medium heat. Lower the heat and simmer until the lentils are cooked but still have a bite, about 20 minutes.

Immediately remove from the heat and drain in a colander, then tip the lentils into a bowl. While they are still warm (so they absorb the flavours better), dress with the sherry vinegar, tamari and your chosen oil. Use as required.

You can keep these lentils in the fridge for up to 5 days, but take them out at least an hour before serving, to bring them back to room temperature.

Sourdough breadcrumbs

I use these all the time – to add colour and texture to food. I am drawn to sourdough breads because of their earthy, slightly fermented taste and wonderful chewy texture. Their crunchy, slightly rough breadcrumbs give many dishes a really strong character. I sprinkle them over salads and warm dishes, and incorporate them into several sauce bases. As a toolbox item, they work in the same way as toasted nuts and braised lentils.

for the sourdough breadcrumbs

½ loaf of good quality sourdough, such as Pain Poilâne

125ml olive oil

sea salt and freshly ground black pepper

Preheat the oven to 190°C/Gas 5. Tear the bread into large chunks, leaving on the crust. Place in a food processor and pulse until you have rough breadcrumbs. Tip into a bowl, add the olive oil, season with salt and pepper and toss to mix.

Tip the breadcumbs on to a baking tray and spread them out well – they need to be well spaced to toast evenly. Place in the oven for 15–20 minutes until golden and crunchy, checking regularly and shaking the pan as you do so, to ensure the crumbs toast evenly.

Allow the breadcrumbs to cool, before using. You can store them in an airtight container for a week or so – they keep well as long as the air doesn't get to them!

Toasted nuts

Nuts lend texture and flavour, giving dishes a rustic quality that I find irresistible. Many are at their peak in the autumn, the season when English cobnuts become available and French walnuts arrive from Périgord. I use good quality nut oils too, preferably cold-pressed as these are more subtle than toasted or heated nut oils.

Apart from scattering toasted nuts on to dishes, I also use them in sauces, such as the one I make using walnuts, anchovy, garlic and sourdough breadcrumbs to serve with grilled veal chops or roasted white fish. Another favourite is the Spanish sauce, Romesco – a pungent rough-textured mix of toasted almonds, dried roasted chillies, garlic and virgin olive oil. I also use ground toasted almonds to thicken some dishes, such as fish and chicken stews.

Freshness is of the utmost importance. Buy nuts in their shells if you can and use them soon after purchasing, as they turn rancid fairly quickly. Nuts in shells need air, so they should be turned, while shelled nuts should be kept in an airtight container in a cool, dark cupboard.

Nuts, like spices, need to be gently warmed through before you use them, in order to release their flavour. There is no specific method to this and individual recipes will tell you how to prepare them. But, as a general guide, you can spread the nuts out on a baking tray and put them in a preheated oven at 180°C/Gas 4 for 3–4 minutes to warm and release their flavour, or allow a little longer for a deeper colour.

Roasted red onions

These beautiful, deep purple rings lend a superb depth of flavour and colour to many cold dishes. Their sharp sweetness sits somewhere in the middle of the scale. *Illustrated on previous spread*

for the roasted onions

5 medium red onions, peeled
100g caster sugar
sea salt and freshly ground black pepper
200ml balsamic vinegar
50ml extra virgin olive oil

Preheat the oven to 180°C/Gas 4. Slice the onions into pinwheels, about 3mm thick, and spread out on a baking tray. Sprinkle with the sugar and a generous pinch each of salt and pepper. Pour over the balsamic vinegar and olive oil and mix together lightly with your hands. Roast in the oven for 30 minutes or so, turning them (with tongs or a wooden spoon) and basting halfway through cooking. When the onions are ready, they should be deep purple in colour and glistening, tasting sweet and sharp at the same time.

Slow-roasted tomatoes

These lend flavour and sweetness to many recipes and I have endless uses for them. Softer and less chewy than sun-dried tomatoes, they work really well with vegetables, fish and red meat, and with cheeses, especially fresh goat's cheeses and ricotta. Warm from the oven, they are delicious with scrambled eggs on toast. They also form the basis of my tomato and chilli jam. I suggest you use plum tomatoes, as they have a good flavour and a pretty shape when semi-dried in this way (San Marzano is an excellent variety). It is most important that they are ripe and in good condition. These slow-roasted tomatoes keep well for several days, or you can store them for longer (up to a month) in sterilised jars, kept covered with a layer of extra virgin olive oil.

for the slow-roasted tomatoes

6 plum tomatoes
10g caster sugar
10g sea salt
10g freshly ground black pepper

Turn your oven on to its lowest possible setting – probably 100°C/ Gas 1/4. Halve the tomatoes lengthways and lay them, cut side up, in a single layer on a large baking tray. In a small bowl, mix together the sugar, salt and pepper, then sprinkle all over the cut surface of the tomatoes. Roast, undisturbed, in the oven for 3–4 hours until they shrivel up – their pointy ends turning up like Turkish slippers. Remove and set aside until ready to use. Slow-roasting intensifies the flavour, giving the tomatoes a deliciously sweet, earthy taste.

Agra-dolce

The principle of agra-dolce is essentially about achieving
balance and harmony from contrasting tastes – salty
(or savoury) and sweet pulling against other, yet
complementing each other completely. It belongs in the
toolbox because it is a concept that I love and one I find
myself using time and time again.

You will come across agra-dolce in most of my recipes,
using the balance of tamari and maple syrup, or fish sauce
and palm sugar, or pickled fruits and salty pungent
cheeses like feta, or young lemony goat's cheese with
tomato and chilli jam or pickled figs, for example.

It takes a while to perfect the principle. Like a set of
old-fashioned scales, the ideal balance lies in the middle,
yet it takes very little (in the way of sweet or salty) to tilt
it out of kilter in either direction. When it is well achieved
agra-dolce creates a strong, clear, harmonious flavour
that is deeply satisfying – notably in slow-cooked dishes,
like Lamb with prunes, chilli, coriander and spice mix
(page 180). The relishes on the following pages use the
agra-dolce principle to perfection.

Tomato and chilli jam

I've included this recipe here because it is one thing that I love to have in my fridge at all times. It has a depth and pungency that I find irresistible and it goes with just about everything – I especially adore it dolloped on to creamy scrambled eggs piled on to grilled sourdough toast for Sunday brunch. It also works brilliantly on top of grilled scallops, grilled lamb chops or rare roast beef – alongside homemade horseradish cream, green beans and little oily black olives.

for the jam

1.5kg Slow-roasted Tomatoes (page 29)

1 tbsp yellow mustard seeds

150ml red wine vinegar

75g peeled fresh root ginger, chopped

7 garlic cloves, peeled and chopped

5 red chillies

140g caster sugar (or 125g palm sugar)

4 tbsp fish sauce

Put the roasted tomatoes into a large saucepan. Toast the mustard seeds in a frying pan over a low heat until they begin to pop. Remove and pound to a fine powder, using a pestle and mortar. Add to the tomatoes along with all the other ingredients.

Place over a very low heat and cook gently for 2 hours, stirring regularly so that the mixture doesn't stick to the bottom. You will at the end have a delicious, inky-stained chutney.

Store in the fridge in a covered bowl for a week or so, or in sterilised jars in a cool place for up to 3 months.

Pickled pear relish

Conference pears are some of the first to appear in the autumn and work well in this delicious relish. It keeps well in the fridge for a week, so you might like to double or triple the quantities, giving you some to serve later on with cheese, cold meats etc. It is especially good with grilled sourdough bread and manchego, creamy dolcelatte and cold roasted lamb. I also serve it with Cauliflower soup with Gorgonzola (page 150).

for the relish

2 tbsp dried cranberries
1 tbsp currants
2 firm, ripe Conference pears
1 Golden Delicious apple
25g unsalted butter
75ml cider or red wine vinegar
2 tbsp caster sugar
3 thyme sprigs (ideally lemon)
1 cinnamon stick
sea salt and freshly ground black pepper

Soak the dried cranberries and currants in a little bowl of warm water for 10 minutes or so – to soften them slightly. Core and chop the pears and apple into small dice (I like to leave the skin on).

Melt the butter in a small pan over a low heat. When it begins to foam, add the diced fruit and cook for 5 minutes until starting to soften. Add all the other ingredients (except salt and pepper) and cook for a further 8–10 minutes. Taste and season, if necessary. Remove the cinnamon and thyme. The relish will have a shiny jewel-like lustre. Serve warm.

You can keep the relish in a covered bowl in the fridge for a week or so, or in a sterilised jar in the fridge for up to a month.

Flavoured yoghurts

I use flavoured yoghurts mostly in conjunction with dishes that have the toolbox spice mix as their foundation. Very often, these dishes are North African or Middle Eastern in feel and their earthy, pungent flavours are well softened by a top hat of yoghurt. It rounds off the flavours, leaving them more palatable and gentle in the mouth.

Thick Greek-style yoghurt is the best kind to use for flavoured yoghurts. It has an unctuous quality and holds additional flavouring much more effectively than thin, light yoghurt.

In the recipes where I've used specific flavoured yoghurts, I have listed their ingredients. The following toolbox recipe is a basic flavour mix that works very well with many roasted meats, pickled vegetables and slow-roasted tomatoes. You could replace the mint with coriander, use a little chopped red chilli instead of Tabasco or add some crushed garlic and/or grated fresh root ginger if you like.

for the flavoured yoghurt

500g thick Greek-style yoghurt

2 tsp Tabasco

grated zest and juice of 2 limes

20 mint leaves, finely chopped

good pinch of sea salt

2 tbsp extra virgin olive oil

In a bowl, mix the yoghurt with the Tabasco, lime zest and juice, chopped mint and salt, then incorporate the extra virgin olive oil, beating well. Cover and refrigerate the yoghurt until ready to use. It will taste pure only for a couple of days.

Season food with care and caution. Salt is probably the most critical of all ingredients in the kitchen. Used wisely it enhances and turns the volume up on an ingredient's natural flavours. Use too little and you are not doing justice to a dish, use too much and the natural beauty of a dish is hidden behind an overpowering and abrasive taste. I always use sea salt.

Mayonnaise bases

Mayonnaise bases work in a similar way to flavoured yoghurts. They round out and complete dishes, adding a complexity to the final flavour. A variety of ingredients can be added to a mayonnaise to make it compatible to what you are cooking, including roasted ground almonds and other nuts, saffron, rosemary, garlic, lemon zest, anchovy, basil oil, even puréed roasted tomatoes. These mayonnaise bases work particularly well with the more Mediterranean flavours of tomato-based dishes. The purest mayonnaise base of all is simply enhanced with lemon juice and zest. This works beautifully with crab, white fish, shellfish and any of the really glorious summer vegetables such as asparagus, broad beans and peas.

I use only extra virgin olive oil when making mayonnaise, but if you find the flavour too intense, substitute half the quantity with sunflower oil. Using a food processor is an almost full proof method. The only trick is to pour the oil really slowly – too quickly and the mayonnaise may split. This is the basic recipe. Of course, you can create many different flavoured mayonnaises. Just remember to add the extra ingredients at the beginning with your egg yolks.

for the mayonnaise

3 organic free-range egg yolks
juice of 1 lemon
2 tsp Dijon mustard
sea salt and freshly ground
black pepper
200ml extra virgin olive oil

Place the egg yolks in a food processor and add the lemon juice, mustard and a good pinch each of salt and pepper. Whiz briefly to combine. Pour the extra virgin olive oil into a jug and then, with the motor running, pour it slowly through the funnel in a fine stream until it is all incorporated and the mayonnaise is emulsified.

If the mayonnaise splits, it can usually be rectified by adding 1 tbsp warm water, then incorporating the rest of the oil. If this fails, pour the split mixture into a jug. Wash and dry the food processor, add a further egg yolk and with the motor running, drip the split mixture in just as if it were the oil, then incorporate the remaining oil.

For saffron mayonnaise, I infuse 15–20 saffron threads in 1–2 tbsp hot water for 10 minutes, then add the saffron and infused liquor right at the start.

To make aïoli, I simply add 3 finely puréed garlic cloves at the beginning, with the mustard and lemon juice.

Vinaigrettes

Because I serve so much food at room temperature, I often use vinaigrettes. Cooked and left to cool to a temperate degree is often the best way to appreciate the complex, natural flavours of many vegetables, fish and meat. Indeed, my favourite way to start a meal is with a *salade composé* – a composition of different seasonal produce brought together with a simple vinaigrette.

I vary vinaigrettes according to the season and the food I am dressing. In summer, I tend to use a simple dressing – perhaps a spoonful of basil oil, a drizzle of olive oil, a squeeze of lemon juice and sprinkling of lemon zest. During the colder months, a dressing with a little more depth and heart is called for and I love to use different nut oils, gently warming them through first.

Where I have used specific vinaigrettes, I have listed the ingredients in the individual recipes. This is a simple, versatile vinaigrette and you can use a different vinegar and/or oil as you like, to alter its character.

for the basic vinaigrette

1 tbsp Dijon mustard
1 tbsp sherry vinegar
sea salt and freshly ground black peppera
200ml extra virgin olive oil
juice of 1/2 lemon

Put the mustard and sherry vinegar into a bowl and add a generous pinch each of salt and pepper. Stand the bowl on a cloth to keep it steady, then gradually whisk in the extra virgin olive oil to emulsify. Lastly squeeze in the lemon juice and whisk to combine. Check the seasoning and set aside until ready to use.

If the vinaigrette separates before you are ready to use it, give it a vigorous whisk and it will re-emulsify.

It is important to understand that when flavours are put together, they need a little time to become acquainted. This certainly applies to sauces, mayonnaises and vinaigrettes. So, wait about 10 minutes before tasting and adjusting the seasoning. Once the ingredients have married, you may find that you need something quite different from what you first suspected, or indeed nothing at all.

Taste is about substance and wholeness... without these components a dish becomes unmemorable. Each and every aspect of a recipe needs to be just right – no element should be ignored, otherwise its final outcome will ultimately feel careless.

Basil oil

This sludgy, verdant sauce lends a vibrancy to many of the dishes that I cook. Its flavour is clean and punchy and it works almost as a cleanser with many dishes, making the ingredients sing. It is definitely a pure, clean note towards the top end of the scale.

for the basil oil

3 large bunches of basil
1 garlic clove, peeled
sea salt and freshly ground
black pepper
200ml extra virgin olive oil

Pull the basil leaves from their stalks and put them into a food processor with the garlic and a good pinch each of salt and pepper. Process until the basil is finely chopped. With the motor running, slowly trickle in the extra virgin olive oil through the funnel and continue to blend until you have a beautiful moss green purée. Leave to stand for a few minutes, then taste and adjust the seasoning.

Pour into a jar, cover and refrigerate until ready to use. This basil oil will keep well in the fridge for up to a week.

When I talk about bunches of herbs in a recipe, I mean just that – old-fashioned, generous bunches – as opposed to the mean-spirited little gathering of leaves to be found in plastic packs in supermarkets. Always think abundantly when you prepare food... the finest cooking is about generosity of spirit!

Flavoured oils

I'm not a fan of shop-bought flavoured oils – I've yet to come across any that I like. They oxidise so easily, losing any clarity of flavour in the process. I therefore make my own, using many different flavourings and the best olive oil I can afford. These oils are best used soon after they are prepared. Chilli, garlic and lemon-infused oils are the ones that I use most often.

Chilli oil

I use this oil to give a dish a gentle kick, not an intense overwhelming heat. I therefore use the large red chillies, which are fairly mild in flavour, and always remove their seeds.

To prepare, halve 4 large chillies lengthways and remove the seeds. Slice lengthways into very fine strips, then cut across into tiny squares (almost mincing the chillies). Place in a bowl, add a pinch of sea salt and then pour over 200ml olive oil. Use within 1 or 2 days.

Garlic oil

I am drawn to strong, clean flavours in food and love the gutsy punch of chopped raw garlic. I'm not afraid to throw raw garlic on to many dishes, especially if its rawness is slightly tempered by a really good quality olive oil. I often fold a spoonful or two of garlic oil into lemon mayonnaise or flavoured yoghurt to give a kick. And a bowl of borlotti or white beans really comes alive if you stir in a spoonful or two just before eating.

To prepare, peel 10 garlic cloves, chop them very finely and place in a bowl with a good pinch of sea salt. Pour over 200ml extra virgin olive oil and stir to combine. Use the oil immediately, or within a day or two.

Lemon-infused oil

This is a fragrant, delicately flavoured olive oil that is lovely spooned over grilled white fish; or used to dress a salad or hot vegetables, such as little potatoes, cauliflower or broccoli; or drizzled on to sourdough toast with slow-roasted tomatoes and a young lemony goat's cheese.

To prepare, use a swivel vegetable peeler to remove the zest from 2 unwaxed lemons in large strips. (This is the easiest way to take the zest thinly, leaving the bitter pith behind.) Warm 200ml extra virgin or good olive oil in a small saucepan over a low heat. Add the finely pared lemon zest and leave over the lowest possible heat for 10 minutes or so to let the delicate citrusy flavour infuse the oil. Take off the heat and leave to cool completely. Use immediately or keep in an airtight container for no longer than a day or two.

Lemon zest

The zesting of a lemon could never be described as a recipe, but this is an ingredient I use so often that it warrants a mention here in the toolbox. Its citrusy sharpness adds a dimension to so much of my food and I often use it as a garnish. For example, it partners finely chopped raw garlic and chopped parsley brilliantly to create gremolata, the classic *osso bucco* garnish that I use to finish many slow-cooked dishes.

Lemon zest works beautifully when tossed into a simple salad whose leaves include basil, mint, chervil and rocket. The addition of grated Parmesan, lemon juice and good olive oil is all that is needed, in my mind, to create a perfect green salad.

The tangy zest also cleans up the flavour of many desserts that would otherwise seem a fraction too sweet. Similarly, it works well to counteract the potentially cloying flavour of pickled fruits. In essence, lemon zest is a simple, quick way to add freshness to your cooking. There is no real secret, just be sure to use the finest holes on your grater and only use the yellow part of the skin. The white pith tends to taste very bitter. Grate your zest as close as possible to the time that you are going to use it, as it will dry out fairly quickly if left out uncovered, or indeed even covered in the fridge overnight.

Top note herbs

While base note herbs form the beginning of many dishes on which you layer other flavours, top note herbs are like the icing on the cake – they complete the dish. My top note herbs are largely summer herbs – basil, parsley, coriander, mint, chervil and rocket – with their sharp clean flavours. These herbs don't tend to hold their flavour through vigorous cooking but must be added very close to the end of a dish, even if only as a garnish, to maintain their clarity and vibrancy.

A few herbs fall into both base and top note categories – parsley (flat leaf and curly) is one, while tarragon is another. Also, coriander roots and stalks can lend base flavour to long-cooked dishes, whereas their leaves lose their character almost the moment they are exposed to high heat. I would rarely use woody, earthy base note herbs to finish a dish. A garnish to my mind should always be light and sing the high notes with its flavours.

THE SEASONS

Spring

I am always thrilled to welcome spring because it brings such an abundance of beautiful produce – rhubarb, apricots, new carrots, beetroot, fennel, chards, morels, broad beans, radishes, sweet herbs and soft, lemony goat's cheeses. It is also the season for early asparagus, sweet peas, young leeks, lobsters, scallops, late oysters and, of course, exquisite spring lamb.

With the exception of early October, there is no more beautiful time to celebrate the seasons. As the clocks return to summertime and the days begin earlier, the land begins to wake up from its long winter sleep. Bulbs flower almost overnight and life appears a little brighter and happier.

Salad of spring vegetables with herbs, pecorino and lemon-infused oil

This is a celebration of the wonderful sweet vegetables that become available during late spring. I grew up in Australia and I love the heat, but there is something so particular and gentle about a warm late spring day in this country. Somehow this salad epitomises everything that is lovely here at this time of the year. If you can't find a young pecorino cheese, use feta instead.

Serves 4

1 bunch of asparagus (about 10 spears)

250g freshly podded broad beans

150g freshly podded young peas

sea salt and freshly ground black pepper

4 tbsp Lemon-infused Oil (toolbox, page 44)

small handful of basil leaves

small handful of mint leaves

handful of rocket leaves

175g young pecorino, thinly sliced

1/4 cup Roasted Red Onions (toolbox, page 29), optional

grated lemon zest, to taste

squeeze of lemon juice, to taste

Place a large pot of well salted water on to boil. Snap the ends off the asparagus. When the water is boiling rapidly, drop in the asparagus and allow to return to the boil, then cook for 45 seconds or until just tender. Remove the asparagus spears from the pan with tongs and put into a colander. Refresh under cold running water.

Now add the broad beans to the pan, allow the water to come back to the boil and cook for 45 seconds, also. Remove with a slotted spoon and tip into a colander, then refresh under cold water. When cool, slip off the dull greenish grey skins to reveal the delicate green beans hidden inside.

To cook the peas, drop them into the same boiling water, return to the boil and cook for 1 minute. Drain and refresh in the same way.

To assemble, gently pat the asparagus, peas and broad beans dry and place in a bowl. Season with salt and pepper and spoon over a little of the lemon-infused oil. Set aside.

Combine the herb and rocket leaves in another bowl. Spoon over a little of the lemony oil, season and toss lightly with your fingers.

To serve, pile the leaves on to a large plate or divide among serving plates. Arrange the pecorino slices, broad beans, peas and asparagus on top, adding the roasted red onion slices too, if using. Drizzle over the rest of the oil and scatter over a few herb leaves. A sprinkling of lemon zest and a squeeze or two of lemon juice would not go amiss.

Morels on toast

Looking almost as though they are mushrooms that belong to another world, morels are wonderful to eat. They are usually around during late February and early March, depending on the weather, though often fearfully expensive. To make the cost a little more bearable, I have paired them with portobello mushrooms here. If you're feeling really extravagant, use all morels! On the other hand, if you're feeling poor, portobellos taste pretty good on their own, treated in this simple way.

Serves 4

500g morels

500g portobello mushrooms

4 slices of chewy peasant-style bread

1 garlic clove, halved

1 tbsp extra virgin olive oil, to drizzle

25g unsalted butter

sea salt and freshly ground black pepper

juice of ½ lemon

1 tbsp Dijon mustard

200ml crème fraîche

1 tbsp very finely chopped curly parsley

Start by cleaning the morels. I use a mushroom brush (though a pastry brush is fine if you haven't got one). Gentle brushing (rather than washing) helps to remove the dirt but not the flavour. Check the morels carefully for bugs. Wipe the portobello mushrooms clean with a damp cloth and break them in half with your fingers.

Toast the bread under a hot grill on both sides. Rub all over with the cut garlic clove and drizzle with extra virgin olive oil.

Melt the butter in a large frying pan. When it is sizzling, add the portobello mushrooms and cook for about 2 minutes. Season generously with salt and pepper.

Add the morels and cook for a minute or so, without stirring. Squeeze over the lemon juice and leave the mushrooms alone once again to cook for another 2 minutes. This results in a lovely, meaty texture (if you stir them continuously, they will stew).

Add the mustard and crème fraîche, stir to combine, then increase the heat to allow the cream to bubble and thicken slightly.

Now, taste and adjust the seasoning – you will probably need a little more salt and pepper. Spoon the mushrooms on top of the toast and sprinkle with finely chopped parsley. Serve straight away!

I season twice during cooking – once in the early stages to tickle and encourage flavours to show themselves, then finally just before serving to pull everything together. I don't season in between because all dishes change in flavour as they are cooking. I like to let them find their own feet in the time in between.

Warm asparagus with herb mayonnaise

Asparagus has a short glorious season straddling late spring and early summer – just 6 weeks from around the beginning of May. I choose to eat it only during its short stay with us, never feeling tempted to buy asparagus grown in foreign climates. There are many ways to enjoy it while it is here.

Serves 4

2 bunches of home-grown asparagus (about 20–24 spears)

sea salt and freshly ground black pepper

Herb mayonnaise

150ml Mayonnaise (toolbox, page 36)

1 tbsp chopped chives

1 tbsp chopped tarragon leaves

1 tbsp finely chopped curly parsley

1 tbsp chopped basil

50ml crème fraîche

To serve

extra virgin olive oil (ideally a gentle kind, such as Ligurian)

lemon wedges

First, prepare the mayonnaise. Stir the chopped herbs and crème fraîche into the basic mayonnaise and adjust the seasoning if necessary. Set aside.

While you prepare the asparagus, put a pot of really well salted water on to boil. Snap the asparagus stalks close to the base to remove their woody ends. Using a swivel peeler, finely peel the skin from the bottom third of the stalks. This might seem an old-fashioned way of presenting asparagus, but I find the pale, greeny white flesh underneath beautiful, especially against the vibrant green of the just-cooked asparagus tips.

When the water is really boiling, drop in the asparagus. Bring back to the boil and cook until just tender – this takes very little time, usually no more than 45 seconds.

Drain the asparagus immediately and place on warm serving plates. Drizzle with a few drops of extra virgin olive oil and serve with the herb mayonnaise and a wedge of lemon on the side.

All green vegetables should be cooked in really well salted water – salty as seawater. This helps to keep their colour vibrant and their taste pure.

Broad beans with mint, ricotta and crisp Parma ham

The feeling of this dish is very light and clean. Crispy, paper-thin sheets of Parma ham lend a lovely, slightly salty-sweet contrast to the spring flavours of broad beans, mint and fresh, sweet ricotta. It is ideal for a light lunch, which I would round off with a bowl of fresh apricots and ginger tea!

Serves 4

500g freshly podded broad beans (about 1kg in the pod)

sea salt and freshly ground black pepper

small bunch of mint, stems removed

75ml extra virgin olive oil, plus extra to drizzle

8 slices of Parma ham

4 slices of good quality bread, (pane toscana or ciabatta)

1 garlic clove, halved

250g fresh ricotta

50g Parmesan, freshly grated

finely grated zest and juice of 1 lemon, or to taste

Preheat the oven to 180°C/Gas 4. Place a pot of well salted water on to boil. When it is boiling steadily, add the broad beans and wait for the water to return to the boil. Cook for a further 20 seconds only. Drain the broad beans and quickly refresh in cold water. Drain well, then peel off the pale greenish grey outer layer, to reveal the tender green beans. Set aside.

Finely chop the mint leaves, saving a few whole leaves for garnish. Put the chopped mint into a bowl with 75ml olive oil, stir well and set aside to infuse for 10 minutes.

Season the broad beans with salt and pepper, drizzle with a little of the mint-infused oil and toss to mix.

Lay the Parma ham slices side by side on a baking tray and sprinkle with a little extra virgin olive oil and black pepper. Place in the hot

oven and roast for 9–10 minutes or until crisp. In the meantime, toast or grill the bread until golden brown. Rub with the cut garlic clove and drizzle with a little extra virgin olive oil.

Put the ricotta into a bowl and fold in the Parmesan, two-thirds of the lemon zest, half of the lemon juice and a drizzle of the minty oil. Season with salt and pepper. Taste and adjust the flavour if necessary – it should be clean, creamy, fresh and vibrant.

Lay the toast slices on individual plates. Spoon the ricotta mixture on to the toast, then pile the broad beans on top. Arrange the crisp, warm, Parma ham on the salad and scatter over a few mint leaves. Spoon on a little more mint-infused oil, sprinkle with the rest of the lemon zest and squeeze over the last of the lemon juice to serve.

Leeks vinaigrette with eggs mimosa, capers and black olives

A timeless classic, leeks vinaigrette makes a lovely starter. I've added eggs mimosa (so-called because they resemble the flower), and capers and olives for sharpness and depth. Sourdough breadcrumbs can also add a delightful textural contrast, or you might prefer to serve some good, crusty, open-textured white bread on the side. Choose small, firm leeks with a good proportion of white flesh. Dress while still warm, as this encourages them to soak up the flavour of the vinaigrette.

Serves 4

20–24 trimmed young leeks, well washed

200ml verjuice (see page 81)

300ml water

8 whole black peppercorns

4 thyme sprigs

3 bay leaves

Vinaigrette

1^{1}/$_{2}$ tsp Dijon mustard

1 tbsp cream

sea salt and freshly ground black pepper

1^{1}/$_{2}$ tbsp red wine vinegar

80ml extra virgin olive oil

To finish

2 organic free-range eggs, hard-boiled

1 tbsp capers preserved in salt, well rinsed in tepid water

handful of black olives (ideally Niçoise or Ligurian)

small bunch of curly parsley, stalks removed and very finely chopped

Check that the leeks are thoroughly clean (they can hold dirt all the way down to the stem). Pour the verjuice and water into a pan (large enough to hold all the leeks) and add the peppercorns, thyme and bay leaves. Place over a medium heat and bring to a gentle boil, then add the leeks. Turn down the heat slightly and simmer gently for 8–10 minutes, or until tender. Meanwhile, make the dressing.

For the vinaigrette, put the mustard and cream into a small bowl, add a little salt and pepper and whisk together. Add the wine vinegar and stir to combine. Now, slowly add the olive oil in a thin steady stream, whisking constantly to emulsify. Set aside for 5 minutes or so, to allow the flavours to get to know each other.

Meanwhile, peel the hard-boiled eggs and grate on the finest holes of your grater – they should have a very light texture.

As soon as the leeks are cooked, remove them from the pan and drain on kitchen paper. Lay them neatly on top of each other on warm plates and spoon over half of the vinaigrette. Scatter the grated eggs, capers and olives randomly on top. Drizzle over the last of the vinaigrette, dust with pepper and sprinkle with chopped parsley to serve.

Spinach soup with nutmeg and crème fraîche

Every time I make this soup, I am excited and dazzled by its beautiful, mossy green colour. Sludgy in texture, it has a fresh, light taste. The trick is to hardly cook the spinach at all, in order to keep its strong, clear colour.

Serves 4

300g young, tender spinach leaves (pousse)

25g unsalted butter

2 banana shallots, peeled and finely sliced

1 garlic clove, peeled and finely chopped

sea salt and freshly ground black pepper

1 litre Chicken Stock (toolbox, page 18)

100ml crème fraîche

1/2 tsp freshly grated nutmeg, or to taste

grated lemon zest, to sprinkle (optional)

Start by washing the spinach really well in several changes of water. Spinach tends to hold dirt, so make sure you wash it until the water runs clear. Drain and shake the spinach dry.

Place a large pan (big enough to hold the spinach) over a medium-high heat. Add the spinach and cook until it just wilts (the water clinging to the leaves after washing generates enough steam for cooking). Drain in a colander and set aside.

Rinse and dry the saucepan. Add the butter and melt gently over a low heat until softly foaming, then add the shallots and sweat for 5 minutes, or until softened and translucent. Add the garlic and cook for a minute or two, then season generously with salt and pepper.

Add the spinach and stir once or twice to combine, then pour in the stock and turn up the heat. Bring to a simmer, then immediately remove from the heat. Purée the soup in a blender, in batches as necessary, until velvety smooth.

Return the soup to the saucepan and stir in the crème fraîche. Add the grated nutmeg, then check for seasoning – adding a little more nutmeg, pepper and/or salt to taste. Reheat gently... there's nothing worse than soup that's not hot enough. I like to add a sprinkling of grated lemon zest before serving.

Celery and leek soup with truffle oil

I am always amazed that so many people say they don't like celery. The inner white heart is one of the finest things I could eat, especially on a warm day, when its delicious watery crunch is so refreshing. The importance of celery in cooking shouldn't be underestimated either, as it has a fundamental role in the making of a good stock and lends character to many slow-cooked dishes.

Serves 4

400g celery, trimmed

2 leeks (white part only)

50g unsalted butter

2 medium or 1 large potato(es), peeled and chopped

2 bay leaves

2–3 thyme sprigs

1 or 2 flat leaf parsley stems

sea salt and freshly ground black pepper

1 litre Chicken Stock (toolbox, page 18)

150ml double cream

truffle oil, to drizzle

Separate the celery stalks and peel them finely, then chop roughly. Wash and chop the leeks. Melt the butter in a large pan over a low heat. Add the celery and leeks and cook gently for 15 minutes or so, until the celery is soft but not coloured.

Add the potato, bay leaves, thyme and parsley and season with a pinch or two of salt and a little pepper. Pour in the stock and bring to the boil, then lower the heat and simmer gently for 20 minutes.

Remove from the heat and discard the herbs. Purée the soup in small batches in a blender, really thoroughly. Pass through a chinois (not a fine-meshed one) back into the pan to ensure a really smooth, creamy texture.

Pour in the cream and reheat gently. Check the seasoning and serve topped with a restrained drizzle of truffle oil.

Another old-fashioned idea of mine is that celery eaten raw should be peeled. It's an attention to detail – like chopping parsley very finely or peeling the end of asparagus – that makes all the difference to a well considered dish.

Baked ricotta with roasted tomatoes, black olives and basil oil

This is a delicious way to serve ricotta and you can cook it a day ahead if it makes life simpler. The flavour is more interesting if you allow it to cool to room temperature – it will also be easier to slice. You can use the baked ricotta slices as a base for a more elaborate antipasti plate – adding salami, bresaola, marinated artichokes and/or grilled pepper, if you like.

Serves 6

olive oil, to brush tin

500g ricotta cheese

2 organic free-range eggs, beaten

225g Parmesan, freshly grated

grated zest of 1 lemon

1 tbsp soft thyme leaves, finely chopped

sea salt and freshly ground black pepper

To serve

about 12 Slow-roasted Tomato halves (toolbox, page 29)

handful of black olives (ideally Niçoise or Ligurian)

90ml Basil Oil (toolbox, page 42)

handful of rocket, tossed in a little lemon juice and olive oil (optional)

Preheat the oven to 150°C/Gas 2. Brush a non-stick 500g loaf tin with a little olive oil.

In a large bowl, whisk the ricotta and eggs together until smooth. Add the Parmesan, lemon zest and chopped thyme. Stir lightly to combine and season with salt and pepper to taste.

Spoon the mixture into the prepared tin, place in a roasting tray and pour in enough water to come halfway up the sides of the loaf tin. Carefully place in the oven and bake for 40 minutes or until the ricotta is firm. Set aside to cool to room temperature.

When cooled, carefully turn out on to a board and cut into slices with a sharp knife. Arrange the slices on individual plates and add a couple of roasted tomatoes, a few black olives and a spoonful of basil oil. Also, a tangle of dressed rocket does not go amiss.

Mezze plate

This plate of different flavours was inspired by a delicious lunch I had in a Moroccan restaurant in Sydney, called Cafe Mint – I strongly recommend a visit if you should ever be passing that way. These dips work beautifully together, or you can serve any of them separately, with other 'bits and pieces' as you like. All of the dips keep well in the fridge for up to 5 days.

Roasted tomato and red pepper purée

This delicious purée has a wonderful rustic quality. It sits happily on the mezze plate, but would also be lovely served with grilled firm-fleshed white fish or chicken.

Serves 4

4 red peppers

2 red onions, peeled and roughly chopped

4 garlic cloves, peeled and roughly chopped

6 plum tomatoes, roughly chopped

2 red chillies, sliced

bunch of coriander, washed

1 tbsp Roasted Spice Mix (toolbox, page 16)

1 tbsp dried mint

1 tbsp extra virgin olive oil

1 tbsp good quality balsamic vinegar

sea salt and freshly ground black pepper

125ml plain yoghurt

1/2 bunch of mint, leaves only

Preheat the oven to 100°C/Gas 1/4. Halve, core and deseed the red peppers, making sure you remove all the white pith and membrane. Put the peppers into a roasting pan with the red onions, garlic, tomatoes and chillies.

Separate the coriander leaves and set aside; finely chop the roots and stems and scatter over the vegetables. Sprinkle with the spice mix and dried mint, then drizzle over the extra virgin olive oil and balsamic vinegar. Season with salt and pepper and toss to mix. Slow-roast in the oven for 40 minutes, stirring occasionally, or until the red peppers are soft and slightly caramelised.

Remove from the oven and allow to cool to room temperature, then whiz in a blender with the yoghurt, mint and coriander leaves until smooth. Taste the purée and adjust the seasoning – it will almost certainly need more salt.

Balsamic vinegar is a particularly special ingredient. I don't mean the cheap imposter found in most supermarkets and delicatessens, but true balsamic vinegar made from a saba base and aged for at least 12 years. This fine product is soft and sweet, viscous in texture, with no hint of acidity. It may be very expensive, but it is worth every penny – 3 or 4 drops is all that you need to take a dish to a different level.

Beetroot purée

This striking, vivid purée is a staple item on our mezze plate. Its zingy, spiciness allows it to stand proudly on its own, too, so it's worth making extra. I love it simply spread on toast, and with griddled scallops. If you buy ready-cooked beetroot, make sure it is plainly cooked, not boiled in vinegar!

Serves 6
1.5kg cooked beetroot, peeled
2 garlic cloves, peeled
1 large red chilli
bunch of coriander, washed
1/2 bunch of mint, leaves only
1 tbsp grated fresh horseradish
1 tbsp Roasted Spice Mix (toolbox, page 16)
3 tbsp good quality balsamic vinegar, or to taste
2 tbsp olive oil
125ml thick Greek-style yoghurt
sea salt

Place the cooked beetroot in a blender with the garlic and chilli. Chop the coriander roots and stems and add to the blender with the coriander and mint leaves, grated horseradish, spice mix, balsamic vinegar and olive oil. Blend really well to a smooth purée.

Add the yoghurt and pulse quickly, just once or twice. Taste for seasoning – the purée will definitely need salt to bring all the flavours together. You may also need a few more drops of balsamic vinegar – it needs a sharp edge.

Chick pea purée

This purée is only really good if all the flavours are strong and clear. It should taste vibrant, not merely like a houmous, so be prepared to adjust the flavours as necessary. Although I most often serve it as part of the mezze, this chick pea purée also works really well with grilled or roast lamb.

Serves 4
250g cooked chick peas
2 garlic cloves, peeled
1 large red chilli
bunch of coriander, washed
bunch of mint, leaves only
juice of 1 lemon, or to taste
1 tbsp tahini paste
2 tbsp Greek-style yoghurt
1 1/2 tsp Roasted Spice Mix (toolbox, page 16)
50ml extra virgin olive oil
sea salt and freshly ground black pepper

Drain the chick peas (rinse as well if using canned ones). Place the cooked chick peas in a blender or food processor with the garlic and chilli. Chop the coriander roots and stems and add to the blender with the coriander and mint leaves. Add the rest of the ingredients and blend to a purée (don't over-process).

Taste and adjust the seasoning, perhaps adding more lemon and a little more salt than you might expect. Salt definitely helps to bring all the flavours together here.

Mezze salad

A simple mixed leaf and herb salad complements the purées perfectly. Of course, you can vary the salad leaves as you like. The light, lemony dressing is subtle, so as not to detract from the other flavours in the mezze.

Serves 4

handful of dandelion leaves

handful of rocket

handful of bull's blood or ruby chard

10 mint leaves

10 basil leaves

small bunch of chervil, leaves only

sea salt and freshly ground black pepper

finely grated zest of 1 lemon

50ml extra virgin olive oil

juice of 1/2 lemon

Wash and pat dry the salad and herb leaves and place in a bowl. Season with a generous pinch of sea salt and a little pepper, then sprinkle with the lemon zest. Drizzle with the extra virgin olive oil and squeeze over the lemon juice. Toss together lightly with your fingers to serve.

Mezze plate

As I arrange the different elements of the mezze on the plate. I like to add a few roasted tomatoes, a little fresh goat's cheese and a scattering of braised lentils, but you could leave the lentils out to keep it simpler if you prefer. A drizzle of basil oil brings it altogether on the plate.

Roasted Tomato and Red Pepper Purée (page 67)

Beetroot Purée (left)

Chick Pea Purée (left)

Mezze Salad (above)

8 Slow-roasted Tomato halves (toolbox, page 29)

4 tbsp soft, fresh lemony goat's cheese or ricotta (optional)

1/2 cup Braised Lentils (toolbox, page 22), optional

Basil Oil (toolbox, page 42), to drizzle

To assemble your mezze, place a large spoonful of each purée on each individual serving plate and pile the dressed salad alongside. Put a couple of roasted tomato halves and a little goat's cheese on top and scatter some braised lentils around, if using. Drizzle with basil oil and serve!

Crab salad with nam jim and mixed cress

Really good fresh crab meat is a rich and pure delicacy that needs to be served as simply as possible and the clean, clear Asian flavours of nam jim work perfectly. This simple, hot Thai dressing also goes well with barbecued seafood and cold sliced rare beef fillet. It is best prepared shortly before using, as the flavours intensify the longer they sit. I have taken the liberty of adjusting the chillies for a gentler taste – the traditional recipe calls for at least five times the amount!

Serves 4

500g freshly prepared white crab meat (ordered from your fishmonger)

handful of mixed cress or wild rocket

1 large, mild red chilli, finely sliced (optional)

Nam jim

2 garlic cloves, peeled

bunch of coriander, roots and stems only, washed

sea salt

1 green bird's eye chilli, chopped

2 tbsp palm sugar

2 tbsp fish sauce

3 tbsp lime juice, or to taste

2 red shallots, peeled and finely chopped

To serve

lime wedges

First make the nam jim (as close to serving as possible). Using a pestle and mortar, pound the garlic and coriander roots and stems with a pinch of salt until well crushed. Add the chilli and continue to pound. Mix in the sugar, fish sauce and lime juice, then stir in the chopped shallots. Before serving, taste and adjust the flavours as necessary, perhaps adding a little more salt or lime juice.

Dress the crab with about 4 tbsp nam jim – enough to give it a clean, clear, sweet, hot flavour, but not too much otherwise you will overpower the delicate taste of the crab. Scatter the mixed cress through, along with the red chilli for an extra kick if required. Serve with lime wedges on the side.

Mixed cress is something I get periodically from Andrew, my vegetable supplier. It includes pea cress, radish cress, shiso (Japanese cress) and garlic shoots. These make a deliciously tangly knot that is visually very beautiful. Mixed cress isn't easy to find, but you could try asking your greengrocer if he could get hold of one or two (if not all) of the varieties. Otherwise peppery wild rocket is a satisfactory alternative.

Wild garlic is one of those special ingredients – a seasonal treasure that I wait for with eager anticipation. When cooked, these beautiful, dark green, delicate leaves have the gentlest, smoothest essence of garlic about them, which marries well with many of spring's abundant ingredients. Ask your greengrocer to order them in for you, or better still hunt for them yourself. They are most commonly found alongside bluebells in woods. Freshly picked and quickly pan-fried in sweet, unsalted butter, wild garlic leaves make a wonderful accompaniment to spring lamb, roasted wild salmon or pan-fried morels and they are delicious with scrambled eggs on toast. You can also eat them uncooked in a simple salad with other leaves, but be warned – the raw leaves have a much stronger, peppery, garlic taste.

I like fish to be cooked through not translucent at the bone and my cooking times reflect this. I serve fillets skin uppermost, so this needs to be crunchy, golden brown and generously seasoned with salt. The flesh underneath must be succulent and just cooked through. Pan-frying fillets, skin side down, without moving until crisp, and finishing them off in the oven is the best way to achieve this.

Pan-fried salmon with wild garlic

Please don't be tempted to use farmed salmon. Wild salmon has a far superior flavour, even compared with organic farmed salmon. Expensive it may be, but if you only eat wild salmon once this season, the memory of it will sustain you until you can afford it again! Here it is served with mellow wild garlic and a fragrant, herby green mayonnaise.

Serves 4

4 wild salmon fillets, about 175g each

sea salt and freshly ground black pepper

2 tbsp olive oil

4 handfuls of wild garlic leaves, gently washed and patted dry

40g unsalted butter

Sauce verte

1 quantity Mayonnaise (toolbox, page 36)

small bunch of chervil

small bunch of tarragon, leaves only

small bunch of chives

2 tbsp crème fraîche

To serve

1 lemon, cut into 4 wedges

Start by making the sauce verte. Have the mayonnaise ready. Chop the herbs together very finely. Add them to the mayonnaise along with the crème fraîche and stir to combine. Taste and add a little more salt and pepper if needed. You should have a sauce that is light and fresh, both in taste and consistency. Set aside until ready to use.

Preheat the oven to 200°C/ Gas 6. Season the fish generously on the skin side and a little less so on the flesh side. Heat one large (or two smaller) non-stick ovenproof frying pans over a medium heat, then add the olive oil. When the pan is really hot (you will see a faint haze begin to rise from the surface), add the salmon skin side down.

Cook for 3 minutes, without turning, until the skin begins to crisp up and you see the flesh lose its translucency close to where it meets the skin. At this point, transfer the pan(s) to the hot oven and allow the fish to cook for a further 1½–2 minutes. (Overcooking salmon quickly dries the flesh and spoils the texture, so time carefully.)

Remove and set aside to rest in a warm place while you quickly cook the wild garlic. Melt the butter in a shallow saucepan over a medium heat. When it just starts to foam, add the garlic and season with a little salt and a generous grinding of pepper. Cook for no longer than a minute, stirring to ensure the leaves are evenly wilted, then remove from the pan.

To serve, place the salmon fillets, skin side up on warm plates and pile the garlic alongside. Spoon over the sauce verte (or hand it round separately if you prefer) and serve with lemon wedges.

Mackerel fillets with roasted tomatoes and horseradish cream

Horseradish works well alongside oily fish. You really need to grate it freshly, though this may bring tears to your eyes! Mackerel needs to be exceptionally fresh to be delicious. Ask your fishmonger to fillet the fish for you – if the fillets are quite large, allow two per person, if small then you will need to allow three. Mackerel also tastes best when it is very hot, so don't let it sit around before serving.

Serves 4
4–6 mackerel, filleted
sea salt and freshly ground black pepper
1 tbsp olive oil
12 Slow-roasted Tomato halves (toolbox, page 29)

Horseradish cream
200ml crème fraîche
1 tbsp freshly grated horseradish
1 1/2 tsp Dijon mustard

To serve
1 tbsp very finely chopped curly parsley
extra virgin olive oil, to drizzle

Start by making the horseradish cream. Put the crème fraîche in a bowl and stir in the freshly grated horseradish and mustard. Season with a pinch of salt and a tiny amount of freshly ground pepper. (If making ahead, cover and refrigerate, but bring back to room temperature before serving.)

Preheat the oven to 200°C/Gas 6. Season the mackerel on both sides, but a little more generously on the skin side. Heat one large (or 2 smaller) non-stick ovenproof frying pans over a medium heat, then add the olive oil. When the pan is hot and lightly smoking, add the mackerel fillets, skin side down, and cook without turning or moving until the skin is golden and crunchy. Put the pan into the hot oven and cook for just under a minute, then remove.

To serve, layer the roasted tomato halves and mackerel fillets on warm serving plates, placing a dollop of horseradish cream on the bottom and top fillets. Sprinkle over the chopped parsley, drizzle a little extra virgin olive oil around the plate and serve immediately.

A non-stick pan is invaluable in any kitchen – especially for pan-frying fish and meat, and for perfect fried eggs. Non-stick pans need to be well looked after. Don't use an abrasive scourer to clean them. I wrap mine in a dry tea towel to protect them while they are stored.

Lobster curry with tamarind, roasted coconut, ginger and coriander

This dish is based upon a style of cooking that is typical along India's southwest coast, though I have added fish sauce and sugar, which are not traditional ingredients. If lobster seems too extravagant, you could use any clean, firm-fleshed fish – monkfish would be perfect.

Serves 4

4 very fresh, live lobsters, about 500g each

sea salt and freshly ground black pepper

3 tbsp vegetable oil

2 onions, peeled and fincly sliced

5cm piece fresh root ginger, peeled and finely diced

4 garlic cloves, peeled and finely chopped

2 red chillies, chopped

1 tbsp coriander seeds, toasted

5 ripe tomatoes, chopped

1 tbsp caster sugar

3 tbsp fish sauce

3 tbsp tamarind water (see page 205)

1½ x 400ml cans coconut milk

75g unsweetened dried coconut flakes, lightly toasted

Bring a large pan of salty water to a fast boil, then drop in the lobsters and cook for 8 minutes. Remove from the pan and leave until cool enough to handle, then extract the meat. Take a sharp knife and make an incision all the way down the middle of the body. Remove the flesh and cut into medallions, discarding the stomach sac and the dark intestinal thread, which runs the length of the body. Crack the large claws with the back of a heavy knife and gently remove the meat. Save the legs for garnish.

Heat the oil in a heavy-based pan over a medium heat. Add the onions, lower the heat a little and cook gently, stirring every now and then, until they are translucent.

Meanwhile, put the ginger, garlic, chillies, toasted coriander seeds and tomatoes in a blender and whiz to a paste. Scrape out the mixture and add it to the onions in the pan. Cook, stirring frequently, for 5 minutes.

Add the sugar, fish sauce and tamarind water and stir well, then pour in the coconut milk. Turn the heat to medium and simmer for 10 minutes. Add the cooked lobster and heat gently for 2–3 minutes until it is just warmed through. Check the seasoning.

Ladle the curry into warm bowls or soup plates and garnish with the reserved lobster legs and toasted coconut flakes to serve.

Buy live lobsters from your fishmonger – they will taste all the better for being so fresh. Order them in advance and check they are still feisty when you collect them. Wrap in damp newspaper, keep in a box and cook soon after buying. The kindest thing to do is pop the lobsters in the freezer for an hour or so before cooking – to put them into a deep sleep. Then, bring a large pot of salty water (as salty as the sea) to the boil. Drop in the sleepy lobsters and cook for 8 minutes exactly.

Rabbit, pancetta and verjuice

I have cooked a lot of rabbit over the past year. I really enjoy its flavour and it proves to be very popular on the restaurant menu. I prefer the taste and texture of farmed, free-range rabbit to that of wild rabbit, which tends to be stronger in flavour, tougher and sometimes riddled with shot. Longer, slower cooking works better for me with rabbit – I like it when the meat is so soft that it falls from the bone. If you prefer firmer flesh, simply reduce the cooking time by half.

Serves 4

1.5kg farmed free-range rabbit, jointed (or ask your butcher for 4 back legs)

sea salt and freshly ground black pepper

2 tbsp olive oil

6 slices of pancetta (or smoked, streaked bacon)

1 large yellow onion, peeled and finely sliced

120ml verjuice (or dry white wine)

2 tbsp Dijon mustard

3 bay leaves

2 thyme sprigs

3 garlic cloves, peeled and finely chopped

300ml Chicken Stock (toolbox, page 18)

2 tbsp crème fraîche

1 tbsp finely chopped parsley

Preheat the oven to 150°C/Gas 2. Season the rabbit generously with salt and pepper. Place a flameproof casserole (large enough to accommodate all the ingredients) over a medium heat and add the olive oil. When it is hot and just smoking, add the rabbit pieces and brown them really well over. As they brown, remove the pieces and set aside.

Add the pancetta and onion to the casserole, turn down the heat and cook for 5 minutes or until the pancetta is browned and the onion has started to soften.

Return the rabbit pieces to the pan, pour over the verjuice and add the mustard. Turn up the heat a little, so the liquor bubbles, then add the bay leaves, thyme and garlic, and pour on the stock. Cover the casserole tightly with foil, place in the oven and cook for 1 hour, 20 minutes. The rabbit should be very, very tender by this stage.

Carefully remove the rabbit pieces and set aside. Place the casserole over a high heat and let the liquor bubble to reduce slightly. You want to thicken it a little and intensify the flavour. This should take no longer than 5 minutes.

Add the crème fraîche and stir to combine with the juices. Return the rabbit pieces to the pan and warm through for a minute or so. Check the seasoning and serve sprinkled with the chopped parsley.

Verjuice is a sour juice extracted from unripe grapes. It lends a special flavour and is available from selected supermarkets and specialist food shops, but if you are unable to find it, use a dry white wine instead.

Char-griddled salt-crusted fillet of beef

I love to eat simply grilled beef fillet with a purée of potatoes and a peppery rocket salad. Crème fraîche spiked with freshly grated horseradish and hot English mustard is also a delicious condiment to serve on the side. Ask your butcher for a really good piece of fillet – look for an intense, deep red colour and an even marbling of fat through the meat.

Serves 4
200g sea salt
2 tbsp freshly ground black pepper
a little vegetable oil, for oiling
1kg prime fillet of beef
2 tbsp extra virgin olive oil
juice of 1 lemon

To serve
Horseradish Cream (page 134)

Sprinkle the salt and pepper on a small baking tray to make an even layer, about 5mm thick. Set the tray aside, close to the hob.

Preheat a griddle or heavy-based non-stick pan and oil very lightly. Cut the beef fillet into 4 thick slices and place on the hot griddle. Cook, without moving for 4 minutes, then turn and cook on the other side, undisturbed, for 4 minutes.

Carefully remove the meat and place on the salt-encrusted tray. Turn the meat once so the seasoning coats both sides, then allow to rest for 15 minutes. (This resting stage is very important – don't skimp on it).

Return the salt-encrusted steaks to the griddle and cook for a further 1 minute on each side for medium to rare meat. Lift the meat back on to the tray and allow to sit for another 2–3 minutes.

Transfer the beef to a board, drizzle with the extra virgin olive oil and squeeze over the lemon juice. Cut into generous slices and arrange on warm plates. Serve with the horseradish cream and accompaniments.

All cooking, for me, relies heavily on the use of beautiful quality ingredients, treated with the utmost respect – sourced from people who care about what they raise and grow. I strongly recommend that you seek out good suppliers if possible. In particular, try to source meat from a local butcher with an excellent reputation.

Lamb cutlets with skordalia and spinach

Little lamb cutlets are delicious griddled or barbecued and served with skordalia – a Greek-style mashed potato, only much more. A good skordalia is garlicky, sharp and tangy, with a texture that is slightly crunchy and creamy all at the same time. It tastes best at room temperature. Ask your butcher for French-trimmed cutlets.

Serves 4

12 best end lamb cutlets

sea salt and freshly ground black pepper

a little vegetable oil, if needed

Skordalia

5 garlic cloves (unpeeled)

100g blanched almonds

3 small-medium Desirée potatoes

finely grated zest and juice of 1 lemon

70ml extra virgin olive oil

To serve

Spinach with Garlic, Lemon and Chilli (page 139)

First, make the skordalia. Preheat the oven to 150°C/Gas 2. Put the garlic cloves on a small baking tray and roast in the oven for about an hour until soft and caramelised. Set aside to cool. Turn the oven up to 180°C/Gas 4. Spread the nuts out on a baking tray and warm in the oven for 3–4 minutes. Allow to cool, then grind very coarsely using a pestle and mortar, or by pulsing in a blender.

In the meantime, peel and chop the potatoes and cook in salted water until soft, about 15–20 minutes. Drain and place in a bowl. Squeeze the soft garlic flesh out of the skins and add to the potato. Mash together until really smooth. Add the ground almonds, lemon zest and juice, a good pinch of sea salt and a grinding of pepper. Stir to combine, then slowly add the extra virgin olive oil in a thin stream, whisking as you do so. Check the seasoning.

To cook the lamb cutlets, preheat your barbecue, grill or griddle pan (oiling it lightly if necessary). Season the lamb cutlets generously on both sides. When hot, place the cutlets on the barbecue or griddle pan (or under the grill) and cook for 3 minutes, then turn and cook for a further 2 minutes.

Place the lamb cutlets on warm plates and serve with the warm spinach and skordalia.

All nuts need warming gently in the oven to release their flavour – just 3–4 minutes is all it takes in a preheated moderate oven to bring out their natural flavour and aroma.

Salad of lamb, green beans and fennel with tomato and chilli jam

One of the sweetest, most tender cuts of lamb is the boned middle loin, also known as the loin, canon, ribeye or strap. It has very little fat, so it is best cooked quickly – either sautéed or grilled. Like all meat, it should be well rested before slicing. A little feta cheese is a good addition to this salad, as a foil for the tomato and chilli jam.

Serves 4

2 boned middle loins of lamb

sea salt and freshly ground black pepper

100g fine green beans, topped but not tailed

2 fennel bulbs, tough outer layer removed

juice of 1 lemon

olive oil, for cooking

4 handfuls of mixed salad leaves

Dressing

1 tsp finely grated lemon zest

juice of 1/2 lemon, or to taste

40ml extra virgin olive oil

1 1/2 tsp freshly grated Parmesan

To serve

4 tbsp Tomato and Chilli Jam (toolbox, page 32)

2 tbsp black olives (optional)

Make sure the lamb is at room temperature. Bring a small pan of salty water to the boil, then add the green beans and blanch for 2 minutes. Drain, refresh under cold running water and set aside. Slice the fennel very finely and immerse in a bowl of cold water with the juice of 1 lemon added to prevent discolouration.

Place a medium (preferably non-stick) frying pan over a medium heat and add a good splash of olive oil. Season the meat very generously with salt and pepper. When the oil is smoking, add the lamb loins and cook for 3 minutes on one side without moving. Then turn and cook for 2 minutes on the other side. (This will give you lamb that is pink in the centre, but not bloody.) Remove from the heat, cover loosely with foil and let it rest for 15 minutes.

While the lamb is resting, wash and pat dry the salad leaves. Place in a bowl and dress with the lemon zest and juice, extra virgin olive and grated Parmesan. Season with a little salt and pepper and add a little more lemon juice if you think it is needed.

To assemble, drain the fennel and pat dry. Cut the meat into 1cm thick slices on the diagonal. Arrange the salad leaves on individual plates and layer the fennel slices, beans and lamb on top. Add a dollop of tomato and chilli jam and scatter a few olives around if you like. Serve at once.

Use your favourite leaves for this salad. I love the combination of beetroot tops, white dandelion leaves, wild rocket, basil and mint leaves, plus sprigs of chervil... but the choice is yours.

Carrots with honey, lemon zest and thyme

Carrots tend to be a little dull simply boiled, but cooking them with honey and butter gives them a deep, caramel flavour and thyme lends fragrance. Chestnut honey, from Italy, will impart a special taste if you can find it. The squeeze of lemon at the finish ensures that the carrots do not end up tasting disproportionately sweet.

Serves 4

8 medium carrots

1¹/₂ tbsp honey

50g unsalted butter

6 thyme sprigs

sea salt and freshly ground black pepper

grated zest and juice of ¹/₂ lemon

finely chopped curly parsley, to sprinkle (optional)

Peel the carrots and cut them into chunky slices on the diagonal. Place in a saucepan and pour on enough cold water to just cover. Add the honey, butter, thyme and a generous pinch of salt. Place over a medium heat and bring to the boil, then lower the heat to a simmer. Cook for 15 minutes or until the carrots are almost tender.

Now, turn the heat up to boil the liquid rapidly until reduced down to a shiny, sweet glaze – there should be 1–2 tbsp of intensely flavoured cooking liquor coating the carrots... nothing more. Squeeze over the lemon juice and check the seasoning. You'll need a turn of the pepper mill and a pinch or two of salt, but no more.

Just before serving, sprinkle over the lemon zest. A scattering of very finely chopped curly parsley would not go astray either.

This simple accompaniment can be served alongside most meat, poultry and game dishes. It goes particularly well with a simple roast chicken.

Almond panna cotta with poached tamarillos

Raw tamarillos have a very sharp flavour that is too tart for my taste, but poach them gently in a sugar syrup and they become gentler, sweeter and much more palatable. They are jewel-like in their beauty and I can think of no prettier fruit when they are poached. Paired with smooth almond creams, they are exquisite.

Serves 4
75g blanched almonds
185ml whole milk
250ml double cream
100g caster sugar
1 vanilla pod, slit lengthways
grated zest of 1 lemon
2 sheets of leaf gelatine (or
1¹/2 tsp powdered gelatine,
see toolbox, page 246)

Poached tamarillos
4 tamarillos
500ml water
225g caster sugar
1 vanilla pod, slit in half
lengthways
1 cinnamon stick
2 bay leaves

Preheat the oven to 180°C/Gas 4. Scatter the almonds on a baking sheet and place in the oven for about 6 minutes to toast very lightly. Allow to cool, then pulse in a food processor to chop roughly (or do this by hand).

Tip the chopped nuts into a saucepan and pour on the milk and cream. Add the sugar and vanilla pod and bring to a gentle simmer, stirring to help dissolve the sugar. Remove from the heat, add the lemon zest and set aside to infuse for 15 minutes.

In the meantime, immerse the gelatine sheets in a bowl of cold water and leave to soften for about 5 minutes.

Return the infused almond mixture to a low heat and bring just to the boil, then take off the heat. Remove the gelatine from the bowl, squeeze out the water, then add to the hot almond cream mixture, stirring to dissolve. Strain into a jug, then pour into 4 dariole moulds (or similar small individual moulds) and allow to cool. Chill for about 2 hours until set, but don't leave the panna cottas in the fridge for too long as they will continue to firm up on chilling.

To prepare the tamarillos, cut them in half lengthways. Put the water, sugar, vanilla, cinnamon and bay leaves into a shallow, wide saucepan and place over a low heat to dissolve the sugar. Then, turn the heat up and bring to a simmer. Add the tamarillos and poach for 5–6 minutes or until they begin to soften and pop out of their skins. Remove from the heat and leave to cool in the poaching liquid.

To serve, dip the base of each mould into warm water for a second or two to loosen the edges, then invert on to a plate to turn out the panna cotta. Arrange the poached tamarillos alongside and spoon a little of the poaching syrup over them. Serve straight away.

Prune and Armagnac tart

This is a truly wonderful, classic French dessert that cannot be improved upon by any modern twists in my view. If I had to choose my last meal on Earth, then this would be the dessert to round it off!

Serves 8–10

250g Pastry (toolbox, page 242, 1/2 quantity)

flour, to dust

300g good quality prunes, such as Agen

30g unsalted butter

2 organic free-range eggs

120g caster sugar

few drops of vanilla extract

1 tbsp orange flower water

5 tbsp double cream

3 tbsp ground almonds

3 tbsp Armagnac, to drizzle

icing sugar, to dust

crème fraîche, to serve

Roll out the pastry on a lightly floured work surface to a large round, about 3mm thick. Using your rolling pin, carefully lift the pastry and drape it over a 25cm flan tin, about 2.5cm deep, with removable base. Press the pastry into the edges and side of the tin, using your fingers and thumbs. Trim excess pastry away from the rim by rolling your pin straight across the top. Prick the base all over with a fork. Place in the fridge to rest for 30 minutes.

Meanwhile, preheat the oven to 180°C/Gas 4. Stone the prunes and place in a bowl. Pour on hot water to cover and leave to soak for 10 minutes to soften, then drain. Melt the butter in a small pan and allow to cool slightly.

Line the pastry case with greaseproof paper and baking beans and bake 'blind' for 15 minutes. Remove the beans and paper and return to the oven for 5 minutes or until the pastry base is golden brown. Remove from the oven and allow to cool. Increase the oven setting to 190°C/Gas 5.

In a large bowl, combine the eggs, sugar, vanilla extract, orange flower water, cream and almonds. Whisk together lightly until evenly blended, then stir in the melted butter.

Place the flan tin on a flat baking tray (to make it easier to take in and out of the oven). Scatter the prunes evenly over the pastry base, then ladle the whisked egg mixture over the top. Carefully place on the middle shelf of the oven and immediately turn the heat down to 180°C/Gas 4. Bake for 25–30 minutes until the custard filling is golden brown on the surface and still slightly wobbly in the centre.

Remove the flan from the oven and while still warm, drizzle with the Armagnac. Serve warm or at room temperature, with a dusting of icing sugar and a dollop of crème fraîche.

Chocolate sorbet

Surprisingly perhaps, this icy cold, incredibly rich dessert works really well at any time of the year. It has an unforgettable silky smooth, luxurious texture. Poached kumquats are a perfect partner — their slightly sharp, citrus flavour cuts through the richness of bitter chocolate, allowing you to eat just a little bit more! These kumquats keep well in a sealed container in the fridge for up to 2 weeks.

Serves 8

250g caster sugar

600ml water

225g good quality dark chocolate (such as Valhrona, minimum 64% cocoa solids)

1 tbsp cocoa powder

Poached kumquats (optional)

1kg kumquats, washed

225g caster sugar

250ml water

Put the sugar and water into a saucepan over a low heat. When the sugar has fully dissolved, bring to the boil, lower the heat slightly and simmer for 5 minutes until the sugar syrup has a slightly viscous consistency. This is important as it helps to give the sorbet its characteristic, glossy texture.

Break up the chocolate and place in a large bowl with the cocoa. Slowly pour on the hot sugar syrup, stirring gently and continuously until the chocolate has melted into the syrup and the mixture is smooth. (The syrup will thicken considerably.) Allow to cool.

Once the sorbet mixture has cooled completely, pour it into your ice-cream maker and churn until thickened, according to the manufacturer's instructions. The texture should be soft.

To prepare the kumquats if serving, cut them in half lengthways. Tip the sugar into a saucepan, add the water and dissolve over a low heat, without stirring. Then, turn up the heat and cook until the syrup begins to thicken, but not yet colour. Add the kumquats, lower the heat and cook gently for 10 minutes. By now, the fruit will have softened considerably and be wonderfully glossy. Remove from the heat and allow to cool.

Spoon the chocolate sorbet into chilled glasses or small bowls, adding a few poached kumquats if serving.

A little Armagnac or amaretto (1–2 tsp) can be added before churning the mixture if you like. This will also lower the freezing temperature, resulting in an even softer, creamier sorbet.

Lemon syllabub

Wonderfully simple in its execution, this delightful dessert requires no technical skill, just willing tastebuds to adjust the flavours if necessary. A little diced stem ginger is a lovely addition if you happen to have any to hand.

Serves 8

200g caster sugar

200ml dry sherry

finely grated zest and juice of 1 lemon

600ml double cream

1–2 tsp finely chopped preserved stem ginger in syrup (optional)

Combine the sugar, sherry, lemon zest and juice in a bowl and stir well. In another bowl, very lightly whip the cream – just enough to thicken it slightly. Gently fold the sherry mixture into the cream until just combined (the addition of lemon and sherry will continue to thicken the cream). At this point, fold in the chopped ginger together with a little of the syrup from the jar if using.

Spoon the syllabub into small glasses and refrigerate for an hour or so, to chill before serving.

Poached loquats with crème fraîche

Loquats – or Japanese medlars as they are also known – are native to China and Japan and grow in the tropics and around the Mediterranean. They are delicious when cooked, but not good eaten raw. Here, I poach them in a vanilla-scented sugar syrup and serve them with crème fraîche. If you cannot find loquats, apricots, which are related, are also delicious poached in this way.

Serves 4–6

1kg loquats (or Japanese medlars)

225g caster sugar

250ml water

2 vanilla pods, slit lengthways

finely pared zest of 1 lemon

crème fraîche, to serve

Cut each loquat in half and prise out the stone in the centre. You also need to remove the fibrous skin surrounding the stone.

Put the sugar, water, vanilla pods and lemon zest into a saucepan. Place over a medium heat to dissolve the sugar, without stirring, then bring to the boil.

Turn down the heat to a simmer and carefully add the loquats. Poach them for 10 minutes until they are soft and cooked through, yet still holding their shape. Remove from the heat and leave to cool in the sugar syrup.

Divide the loquats among glass serving bowls and spoon over some of the sugar syrup. Serve with crème fraîche.

Summer

I grew up in Australia where summers could be fierce, with endless days on the beach and long, hot restless nights. English summers are very different, but I have learnt to love them none the less. Gentler, sweeter, light filled days, rich green hills and a lazy ripe anticipation in the air.

The produce during these months is glorious – strawberries, raspberries, redcurrants, peaches, nectarines, apricots, courgettes, summer savory, beetroot, peas, broad beans, wild salmon, crab and lobster are among the finest. I love salads and at this time of year leaves are at their best, especially bull's blood, dandelion, watercress, rocket and wonderfully fragrant herbs including tarragon, basil and chervil. Beautiful sweet, ripe tomatoes arrive from Italy to supplement home-grown varieties. With such a bountiful selection, to cook in summer is pure joy.

Chilled almond soup

Known as *ajo blanco* in Spain, this beautiful soup is surprisingly punchy and satisfying. I created this version for an event we shared with the Slow Food movement at Petersham in the summer of 2005, celebrating the use of flowers in the cooking of the Levant. It was, for me, a perfect day!

Serves 4

150g really good quality day-old bread

225g shelled almonds (in skins)

3 garlic cloves, peeled

1½ tbsp sherry vinegar

220ml extra virgin olive oil

sea salt and freshly ground black pepper

375ml ice-cold water (approximately)

To serve

1 perfectly ripe fig

1 tbsp rose syrup, or extra virgin olive oil, to drizzle

1 tbsp finely chopped parsley (optional)

Remove the crust from the bread, then cut into cubes and place in a bowl. Add cold water to cover and allow to soak for 2–3 minutes, then squeeze out excess water and set aside.

Drop the almonds into a pan of boiling water and leave for a minute or two, then remove. When cool enough to handle, slip the nuts out of their skins.

Put the garlic, almonds, bread, sherry vinegar and extra virgin olive oil into a food processor or blender and blend until smooth. Season with salt and pepper. Then, with the motor running, slowly pour in the ice-cold water until the soup is the thickness of double cream. The consistency is very important – too thick and it would feel cloying, too thin and it would be unsubstantial. Pour into a bowl, cover and refrigerate for an hour or longer, until really well chilled.

Ladle the soup into soup plates. Cut the fig into thin wedges and lay two of these in the centre of each bowl. Drizzle with a tiny amount of rose hip syrup, or extra virgin olive oil if you prefer. I like to scatter over some finely chopped parsley to serve.

Parsley soup

I love using herbs in my cooking and parsley is one of my favourites. Although it may appear old-fashioned, many of the dishes I serve are topped with parsley – chopped as finely as it possibly can be. For me, it is the perfect finish and gives a plate a delicate beauty like nothing else. Parsley takes centre stage in this simple clean-tasting soup. It is an ideal start to a meal on a summer's evening.

Serves 6

2 generous bunches of curly parsley

sea salt and freshly ground black pepper

50g unsalted butter

2 leeks (white part only), well washed and chopped

1 medium-large potato, peeled and chopped

1–2 garlic cloves, peeled and chopped

1 litre Chicken Stock (toolbox, page 18)

150ml double cream

Wash the bunches of parsley well – especially the stems, which can retain quite a lot of dirt. Put a large pan of well salted water on to boil and set aside one of the parsley bunches (for blanching). Chop the other bunch roughly.

Melt the butter in another saucepan over a low heat, then add the chopped leeks and sweat for 2–3 minutes or until starting to soften. Add the chopped parsley, along with the potato and garlic and continue to sweat for another 5 minutes. Season with salt and pepper, then pour in the chicken stock. Bring to the boil and simmer gently for 20 minutes.

Meanwhile, drop the other bunch of parsley into the pan of boiling water and blanch for 15 seconds only. Remove and immediately refresh in a bowl of iced water (to retain its intensity and give the soup a beautiful colour).

When the potatoes are really tender (almost falling apart), remove the pan from the heat. In batches, purée the soup in a blender, adding some of the blanched parsley in with each batch. Blitz for a good minute or two – you want the soup to be very smooth.

Finally, return the soup to the saucepan and place over a medium heat. Stir in the cream, taste for seasoning and adjust if necessary, then serve. If you have any left over, this soup will sit happily for a day or so in the fridge.

For a smooth finish

you really need to use a blender to purée this soup. A food processor will not give you such a fine result. If you do not have a blender, use a food processor, then strain the soup through a chinois to ensure a smooth texture.

Spinach, fennel and asparagus salad

I created this salad for a party given by Tate Modern to celebrate the re-hanging of their permanent collections. Held in the spring, the theme was growth and renewal, so I decided that the food should be as strong and as simple as possible – focusing on the season's beautiful produce. It was served as a course on its own, but it is also a lovely accompaniment to grilled fish. *Illustrated on previous page*

Serves 4

150g young, tender spinach leaves (pousse)

1 fennel bulb

6 asparagus spears

sea salt and freshly ground black pepper

40ml extra virgin olive oil

finely grated zest of 1 lemon

1 tbsp finely grated Parmesan

juice of 1/2 lemon

Wash the spinach thoroughly in several charges of cold water. Place in a large saucepan with just the water clinging to the leaves after washing and cook over a high heat until just wilted. This takes very little time – no longer than a minute – don't overcook it. Drain the spinach and set aside to cool.

To prepare the fennel, slice off the base and remove the fibrous outer leaves, then cut the bulb in half lengthways. Place each half, cut side down, on the chopping board and cut lengthways into fine shards, using a very sharp knife – the slices should be almost paper-thin.

Snap off the woody ends of the asparagus and using the same sharp knife, slice the spears finely lengthways. (Shaved raw asparagus has an interesting texture and excellent taste.)

Squeeze out as much moisture from the cooled spinach as possible (but don't be so brutal that you bruise the leaves). Put the spinach into a large bowl and season with a little salt and pepper. Add the extra virgin olive oil and toss through with your hands – the spinach will absorb the oil and take on a luxurious, glossy quality.

Add the fennel shards, asparagus, lemon zest, Parmesan and finally the lemon juice. Toss very gently with your fingertips – you want to create a feeling of space and air. Taste for seasoning, adding a little more salt if needed. Pile the salad on to plates and serve.

When I compose a salad, I like to think about every element. First I look at the season – what is around and at its best. Seasonal foods naturally work well together. Then I think about colour, texture and taste – bitter or sweet, gentle or peppery… always looking to create an interesting balance.

Salad of lentils, avocado and goat's cheese

This salad really epitomises the way I cook. It is certainly an example of how the toolbox works and of how I like to eat. I'm not sure whether growing up in Australia has shaped my food preferences, but I crave earthy, clean, strong flavours!

Serves 4

1 cup Braised Lentils (toolbox, page 22)

2 ripe avocados

juice of 1/2 lemon

12 Slow-roasted Tomato halves (toolbox, page 29)

200g tangy, fresh goat's cheese

100g Roasted Red Onions (toolbox, page 29)

sea salt and freshly ground black pepper

4 tbsp Basil Oil (toolbox, page 42)

extra virgin olive oil, to drizzle

Divide the lentils among serving plates. Halve, stone, peel and slice the avocados, then toss in the lemon juice to prevent discolouration. Layer the roasted tomatoes, goat's cheese, avocado slices and red onions on top of the lentils, alternating them and seasoning here and there with a little salt and pepper as you build. Spoon over the basil oil and finish with a drizzle of extra virgin olive oil.

I love the toolbox flavours here – the earthy, nutty lentils with a hint of sharpness from their dressing, the intense roasted tomatoes and deep purple onions – both sweet and sharp at the same time – all brought together with the vibrant basil oil. Serve as a starter, or as a light lunch with some good peasant-style bread on the side.

Vary this salad by interchanging some of the ingredients. You could replace the goat's cheese with a slice of grilled wild salmon or poached chicken, for example. Or add blanched asparagus or cubed roasted beetroot, or perhaps finely sliced celery heart, shaved fennel or blanched green beans, or a handful of toasted nuts for crunch... the possibilities are endless.

Peppers Piedmontese

I've prepared this dish on and off for over 20 years, ever since I first ate it at Roger Verge's Le Moulin De Mougins in Provence with my father. It was my first Michelin 3-star experience and the most wonderful meal. In essence, it is an uncomplicated dish. I have added mozzarella, roasted onions and basil oil, because for me, along with some good bread, it then becomes a perfect and complete lunch.

Serves 4

8 ripe tomatoes

sea salt and freshly ground black pepper

4 red peppers

12 basil leaves

4 garlic cloves, peeled and finely sliced

6 good quality canned anchovies in oil, drained and cut into small pieces

2 tbsp extra virgin olive oil, to drizzle

2 balls of good quality buffalo mozzarella or *fiore di latte* (an outstanding cow's milk mozzarella)

about 12 little black olives (ideally Niçoise or Ligurian)

100g Roasted Red Onions (toolbox, page 29)

2 tbsp Basil Oil (toolbox, page 42)

First, you need to skin the tomatoes (tedious perhaps, but necessary here). So, place a large pan of salted water on to boil. Using a small paring knife, remove the core from each tomato, then turn upside down and mark a small cross on the base. Drop the tomatoes into the boiling water. Almost immediately (as long as the tomatoes are ripe) the skin will begin to peel back, like the petals of a flower. Remove at once with a slotted spoon and leave to cool slightly.

Preheat the oven to 180°C/Gas 4. Halve the peppers lengthways and remove the core, seeds and white pith. Lay the pepper halves, skin side down, in a shallow baking tray that will hold them comfortably.

When the tomatoes are cool enough, peel, halve and remove the seeds using a teaspoon, then very roughly chop the flesh. Tear the basil leaves into pieces.

Fill the pepper halves with the pieces of tomato, garlic slices, torn basil leaves and chopped anchovies. Drizzle with the extra virgin olive oil and season well with pepper (not salt at this point, as the anchovies may well provide all that is needed). Bake in the oven for 35 minutes or until the peppers are soft and slightly blackened around the edges, but still holding their shape.

Check the seasoning and allow the roasted peppers to cool – room temperature is the ideal warmth to really appreciate the summery flavours of this dish.

Arrange the peppers on a big oval plate so everybody can help themselves, or on individual plates if you prefer. Tear the mozzarella into pieces with your hands and scatter over the peppers, along with the olives and roasted red onions. Spoon over the basil oil to serve.

Aubergines are at their best during the summer months, although you can buy them throughout the year. Look for aubergines with firm, glossy skins that feel heavy in the hand.

Baked aubergines with tomatoes, tarragon and crème fraîche

I love this dish because it sings of summer. Served just warm with nutty brown rice, garlicky yoghurt and a rocket salad on the side, it makes a lovely vegetarian supper. It also works really well with grilled or barbecued lamb.

Serves 4–6

1.5kg aubergines, trimmed

sea salt and freshly ground black pepper

olive oil, to shallow-fry

50g unsalted butter

1kg ripe tomatoes, roughly chopped

4 garlic cloves, peeled and sliced

400ml crème fraîche

2 tbsp tarragon leaves, finely chopped

2 tbsp chopped flat leaf parsley, plus extra to finish

1/2 tbsp chopped thyme leaves (ideally lemon thyme), plus sprigs to garnish

1 tbsp finely chopped chives

50g Parmesan, freshly grated

extra virgin olive oil, to drizzle

Slice the aubergines into 1cm rounds. Lay in a colander and sprinkle generously with salt. Leave to degorge the bitter juices for about 30 minutes – beads of moisture will appear on the aubergine flesh. Before cooking, pat each aubergine slice dry with kitchen paper.

Heat a 1cm depth of olive oil in a large, fairly deep frying pan over a medium-high heat. Fry the aubergine slices, a few at a time, until golden brown on one side, then turn and brown on the other side. Remove and drain on kitchen paper.

Melt the butter in another saucepan. Add the chopped tomatoes and garlic slices and season with a good pinch of salt and some pepper. Cook over a low heat for about 15 minutes until the tomatoes are soft.

Meanwhile, put the crème fraîche into a small pan and bring to the boil over a medium heat. Allow to bubble until reduced by a third, then take off the heat and add the tarragon, parsley, thyme and chives. Add half of the Parmesan and taste for seasoning.

Preheat the oven to 180°C/Gas 4. Line the bottom of a large, shallow ovenproof baking dish with a layer of aubergine slices. Follow with a thin coating of the tomato sauce and a sprinkling of Parmesan. Continue layering in this way, finishing with tomato sauce. Pour over the crème fraîche and sprinkle with the remaining Parmesan. Leave the dish to sit for a few minutes to allow the flavours to get acquainted with each other.

Place in the oven and bake for about 20–25 minutes until golden brown. Allow to stand for 5 minutes or so. Drizzle with a little extra virgin olive oil and sprinkle with a pinch or two of salt. Scatter over some finely chopped parsley and thyme sprigs to garnish and serve... but not too hot!

Braised artichokes with fennel, tomatoes, olives and preserved lemon

This is a vegetable dish that really holds its own. It is a lovely way to serve globe artichokes, undoubtedly the most beautiful member of the thistle family. Deeply nourishing, with sage lending warm base note tones, it is a perfect dish for a cooler summer's evening.

Serves 4

2 heads of fennel

1 lemon, halved

1 tbsp olive oil

25g unsalted butter

sea salt and freshly ground black pepper

2 globe artichokes

2 bay leaves

3 tsp chopped sage, plus extra leaves to garnish

2 garlic cloves, peeled and finely chopped

1 dried red chilli

small pinch of saffron threads

4 good quality ripe tomatoes (preferably plum)

1/2 preserved lemon, chopped

100ml Chicken Stock (toolbox, page 18)

about 12 little black olives (ideally Niçoise or Ligurian)

2 tbsp Basil Oil (toolbox, page 42), or to taste

freshly grated Parmesan, to serve

Preheat the oven to 180°C/Gas 4. Trim the fennel and cut off the base, then remove the fibrous outer layer. Cut each fennel bulb into quarters and squeeze over a little lemon juice.

Place a heavy-based saucepan over a medium heat, add the olive oil and butter and heat until the butter has melted. Add the fennel, season with a little salt and cook for 10 minutes or so.

Meanwhile, prepare the artichokes – a sharp knife is imperative. Lay each artichoke on its side on a board, then cut off the top third and discard. Cut off the stalk and trim all the way around the base until you come to the choke – you should now just be left with the heart. Cut the artichoke heart in half and, with a small paring knife, remove the spiky, fibrous inner choke. Quickly rub the artichoke hearts with the cut lemon to prevent discolouration.

Add the artichoke hearts to the fennel along with the bay leaves, sage and garlic. Crumble in the dried chilli and saffron and stir to combine. Roughly chop the tomatoes and add to the pan, along with the preserved lemon, then pour in the chicken stock. Cover and cook in the oven for 40 minutes or until the fennel is very tender, adding the olives for the last 5 minutes.

Taste and adjust the seasoning then spoon over the basil oil and scatter over some sage leaves to garnish. Sprinkle with grated Parmesan and serve.

Tea-smoked fillets of wild salmon with pickled cucumber salad

Tea-smoking works really well with all oily fish, but especially with salmon – the delicate flavours complementing each other perfectly. I like to use a fragrant heady tea for smoking, such as Lapsang or Yunnan, but experiment to find out which ones you like best. The salmon can be tea-smoked the day before and kept overnight in the fridge if that's more convenient.

Serves 4

1 quantity Tea-smoking Mixture (toolbox, page 20)

4 wild salmon fillets, about 175g each

Cucumber salad

1 large cucumber, peeled and finely sliced on the diagonal

2 tsp sea salt

Dressing

juice of 2 limes

1¹/2 tsp sugar

1 tbsp fish sauce

1 tbsp chopped coriander leaves

1 tbsp finely chopped mint leaves

1 garlic clove, peeled and finely chopped

1 red chilli, deseeded and finely diced

2 drops of sesame oil

To serve

1 quantity Mayonnaise (toolbox, page 36)

Prepare the tea-smoking mixture and set up the tea-smoking equipment as described in the toolbox. Tea-smoke the salmon fillets according to the toolbox instructions, cooking them for 3 minutes. Turn off the heat and leave the salmon to sit in the baking tin with the lid on for a further 3–4 minutes. Remove the lid, take out the fish and set aside until ready to serve.

For the salad, peel the cucumber and cut into fine slices on the diagonal. Sprinkle with the sea salt, tossing gently with your fingers to distribute evenly. Place the slices in a colander and leave to stand for an hour.

To make the dressing, whisk all the ingredients, except the sesame oil, together in a bowl. Finally add the sesame oil.

Rinse the cucumber very lightly under cool water and pat dry with a clean, dry tea towel. Place in a bowl, drizzle over the dressing and toss gently to combine.

Place the tea-smoked salmon fillets on serving plates and pile the cucumber salad alongside. Hand the mayonnaise around separately in a bowl.

Crab claws with chilli oil and mayonnaise

This is hardly a recipe at all – just a combination of delicious things to share! I love food that you have to work a little harder at to eat – it creates a sense of congeniality and community – shared food in the middle of the table is my preferred way of eating. A good fishmonger will be happy to provide you with beautiful, freshly cooked crab claws.

Serves 4

12–16 freshly cooked crab claws (3–4 per person)

1 quantity Chilli Oil (toolbox, page 44)

1 quantity Mayonnaise (toolbox, page 36)

1–2 lemons, cut into wedges (for squeezing over the crab)

little bowls of sea salt

basket of chewy peasant-style bread

small bowl of radishes (optional)

Crack the crab claws gently with the back of a heavy knife, without crushing the meat. Pile them on to a platter. Place on the middle of the table, along with all the other ingredients. Provide finger bowls for everyone, too. Bon appétit!

Beautiful bread is an important part of any meal, though it has its place. Offering a large basket at the beginning of a meal encourages people to fill up too early, lessening their enjoyment of the food to follow, so bear this in mind. Choose breads with character – open textured with a chewy crust. I particularly like sourdoughs and ryes – breads that hold their own and add their particular dimension to a meal.

Squid and chorizo with black olives and red pepper

This lovely inky, unctuous stew is very satisfying to eat, especially when served with garlicky, chewy toast. I have at different times varied the ingredients, adding large cubes of potato, blanched kale or spinach, even substituting the chorizo with mussels or clams. A dollop of saffron mayonnaise or a spoonful of lemon-infused or basil oil stirred in at the end gives the dish a wonderful vibrancy.

Serves 6

1kg baby squid

400g chorizo sausage

4 tbsp olive oil

1 yellow onion, peeled and diced

2 carrots, peeled and finely diced

1 celery stick, diced

3 garlic cloves, peeled and crushed

3 thyme sprigs

4 bay leaves

1 small dried red chilli

sea salt and freshly ground black pepper

finely pared zest of 1 orange

1 red pepper, halved, cored, deseeded and cut into strips

350ml red wine

400g can good quality chopped tomatoes

about 12–18 little black olives (ideally Niçoise or Ligurian)

To serve

4–6 slices of chewy, peasant-style bread

1 garlic clove, halved

Clean the squid by pulling the tentacles and head from the body. Cut the tentacles from the head, discarding the head. Remove the transparent quill from the body and the soft, gooey matter. Rinse the body pouch and tentacles gently under cold running water, drain and set aside. Slice the chorizo on the diagonal into 1cm thick slices.

Heat 3 tbsp olive oil in a deep, heavy-based saucepan. Add the onion, carrots, celery, garlic, thyme and bay leaves. Crumble in the dried chilli and season with a good pinch of sea salt. Twist the orange zest with your fingers (to release its fragrance) and drop into the pan. Cover and sweat over a very low heat for 15 minutes, stirring occasionally. Add the red pepper and sweat for a further 5 minutes.

Pour in the wine and turn up the heat so that it bubbles and reduces slightly. Add the chopped tomatoes, stir well and cook uncovered for 10 minutes. The idea is to reduce the sauce and intensify the flavour.

Meanwhile, heat 1 tbsp olive oil in a frying pan. When smoking, add the chorizo slices and brown quickly on both sides. Tip straight into the tomato mixture, along with the orange, smoky-flavoured oil. At this point, add the olives and simmer for a minute or two. Check the seasoning – you will probably need just a little black pepper and perhaps a small pinch or two of salt – just to bring it all together.

Pour off excess oil from the frying pan, then place over a high heat. In small batches, quickly brown the squid in the very hot pan for no more than a minute, then drop them straight in the inky stew.

Turn off the heat while you grill the bread on both sides. Rub the toast slices with the cut garlic clove. Ladle the stew into warm bowls, discarding the herbs and orange zest. Serve straight away, with the hot garlicky toast.

Red mullet with fennel and saffron mayonnaise

If possible, look for red mullet that are no bigger than your hand and allow two per person. If you can only find medium-sized fish, then allow one each. They should be vibrant rosy pink in colour – shot through with gold flecks. Ask your fishmonger to scale and gut the fish for you.

Serves 4

8 small red mullet, or
4 medium ones
5 black peppercorns, crushed
1 orange, halved
4 bay leaves, plus extra to
garnish if you like
200ml extra virgin olive oil
3 small, smooth fennel bulbs
50g unsalted butter
sea salt and freshly ground
black pepper
juice of 1 lemon

To serve
Saffron Mayonnaise (toolbox,
page 36)

Place the red mullet side by side in a dish and prick the skin here and there with a needle. Sprinkle with the crushed peppercorns and squeeze over the orange juice. Add the bay leaves and pour over 150ml of the extra virgin olive oil. Cover and leave to marinate for 3–4 hours in a cool place (preferably not the fridge).

Trim the fennel and cut into quarters. Roughly chop a few of the feathery fronds and set aside. Melt the butter in a sauté pan. When it is foaming, add the fennel and season with a little salt and pepper. Sweat gently for 3 minutes, then add the lemon juice.

Add water to cover and turn the heat up until the liquor is bubbling. Pour in the remaining 50ml extra virgin olive oil and cook for about 15 minutes until the fennel is really tender and the liquor is well reduced. Check the seasoning and set aside.

Remove the red mullet from the dish, reserving the marinade, and pat dry. Season the fish with salt and pepper.

Heat 3 tbsp of the marinade in a large frying pan. When hot, add the red mullet (you will probably need to cook them in two batches). Allow 2 minutes each side for little mullet, about 3 minutes each side for larger fish (it is important that they remain moist).

To serve, divide the fennel among warm plates and lay the fish on top. Add a dollop of saffron mayonnaise or hand round separately in a bowl. Sprinkle with a little chopped fennel frond and garnish each plate with a sprig of bay leaves if you like. Serve at once.

Monkfish and clams with roasted almonds, rosemary and aïoli

In France, monkfish is known as poor man's lobster. Plump, white and firm, with only a backbone, it is easy to fillet and its meaty texture works well in fish stews. Here you can use mussels or prawns instead of clams, perhaps adding a handful of black olives, or leaving out the almonds... it's up to you. I serve it with garlicky sourdough toast and a leafy salad dressed with lemon and olive oil.

Serves 4

4 tbsp olive oil

2 large red onions, peeled and thinly sliced

sea salt and freshly ground black pepper

about 25 saffron threads

250ml boiling water

2 fennel bulbs

2 dried red chillies

4 rosemary sprigs

2 bay leaves

4 garlic cloves, peeled and finely chopped

1 tbsp sherry vinegar

250ml dry white wine

2 x 400g cans good quality chopped tomatoes

75g blanched almonds

1kg monkfish, skinned, filleted and cut into generous chunks

40 clams, scrubbed clean

To serve

4 slices of sourdough bread

1 garlic clove, halved

Aïoli (toolbox, page 36) or Rosemary and Almond Aïoli (page 221)

Heat the olive oil in a large heavy-based saucepan over a medium-low heat, then add the onions with a pinch of salt and cook gently for about 5 minutes until soft. Put the saffron in a small bowl, pour on the boiling water and set aside to infuse. Preheat the oven to 180°C/Gas 4.

In the meantime, prepare the fennel. Slice off the base and remove the fibrous outer leaves, then finely slice lengthways and add to the onions. Crumble in the dried chillies and add the rosemary, bay leaves and garlic. Cook for a further 10 minutes until the fennel has started to soften.

Now add the sherry vinegar, white wine and saffron together with its water. Allow the liquor to bubble away for a couple of minutes, then add the tomatoes. Give the mixture a good stir, turn down the heat and cook gently for 20 minutes or so. The flavours need time to adjust to each other.

In the meantime, lightly toast the almonds on a baking tray in the oven for 3–4 minutes to release their flavour. Coarsely grind the toasted nuts, using a pestle and mortar, or blender.

Stir the nuts into the tomato mixture – they give the dish a lovely textural quality as well as a delicious nutty flavour. Check the seasoning... you will definitely need to add salt and pepper. (The dish can be prepared ahead to this point.)

About 5 minutes before serving, bring the tomato mixture to the boil. Add the monkfish and clams and simmer for 4 minutes or until the clams have opened and the monkfish is firm to the touch and white in colour. Discard the herbs.

Meanwhile, grill the bread on both sides and rub with the cut garlic clove. Serve the fish stew with the toast, a bowl of garlicky aïoli and a simple salad.

Buy shellfish as
close as possible to
cooking and keep cool.
Mussels and clams are
happiest immersed in
a bowl of really well
salted water in the
fridge until you are
ready to cook them.

Pan-roasted chicken with lentils, roasted tomatoes and basil oil

Chicken supremes are simply chicken breasts with the wing tips attached. I always think they taste better... and you have the added pleasure of being able to gnaw on the bone. Don't be put off at first glance by the number of toolbox components in this recipe – remember that just about every item in the toolbox lasts well in the fridge for up to a week.

Serves 4

2 cups Braised Lentils (toolbox, page 22)

250ml Chicken Stock (toolbox, page 18)

2 tbsp tamari (or soy sauce)

4 organic, free-range chicken supremes

sea salt and freshly ground black pepper

1 tbsp olive oil

8–12 Slow-roasted Tomato halves (toolbox, page 29)

2 tbsp Basil Oil (toolbox, page 42)

4 tbsp Aïoli (toolbox, page 36)

finely chopped curly parsley, to finish

Preheat the oven to 200°C/Gas 6. Place the lentils in a saucepan, pour over the chicken stock and bring to the boil. Turn down the heat, add the tamari and simmer for 2 minutes. Keep warm.

Meanwhile, season the chicken supremes with salt and pepper. Place a large ovenproof (preferably non stick) pan over a high heat. Add the olive oil and when it is hot and just starting to smoke, lay the chicken breasts in the pan, skin side down. Cook without moving (resist the temptation) for 4 minutes until the skin is golden brown. Without turning the supremes, put the pan into the oven (or you could transfer them to a roasting tray). Roast, skin side down, for a further 8 minutes or until the breast feels firm when you press it with your fingers. Remove from the oven and leave to rest in a warm place for 5 minutes or so.

Divide the warm lentils among warm plates. Place a few roasted tomatoes and a chicken supreme on top of each portion and drizzle the basil oil over the lentils. Add a dollop of garlicky aïoli (or pass around separately in a bowl you prefer). Finish with a sprinkling of chopped parsley.

The most vital
ingredient in
any dish is the
attitude you bring to
it. Love and passion
make for a happy
cook… and food
with soul.

Vitello tonnato with tomatoes, olives and basil oil

Vitello tonnato is a classic Italian dish – perfect on a summer menu. It works equally well as a simple one-course lunch or as a part of a buffet. Its beauty lies in the contrast of the sweet, delicate veal against the creamy intense sauce. I've seen other meats used in place of veal, but I don't think anything else works as well. The meat is poached rather than roasted, to keep it moist and tender.

Serves 6–8

Poached veal

1.5kg piece free-range topside of veal

1 yellow onion, peeled and quartered

3 celery sticks, chopped

2 carrots, peeled and chopped

4 bay leaves

small bunch of flat leaf parsley

8–10 peppercorns

Tuna mayonnaise

200ml Mayonnaise (toolbox, page 36)

200g can fine quality tuna, drained

2 tbsp lemon juice

2 tbsp capers (packed in salt), well rinsed and drained

3 fine quality canned anchovy fillets in olive oil, drained

freshly ground black pepper

To assemble

3 ripe tomatoes

2 handfuls of rocket

squeeze of lemon juice

few drops of olive oil

2 tbsp little black olives (ideally Niçoise or Ligurian)

1 tbsp capers, rinsed and drained

3 tbsp Basil Oil (toolbox, page 42)

Half-fill a cooking pot or heavy-based saucepan (large enough to hold the veal) with water. Add the onion, celery, carrots, bay leaves, parsley and peppercorns (but no salt). Bring the water to the boil, then add the veal joint. There should be sufficient water to cover the meat – if not, add enough to do so. Turn the heat down to a steady, gentle simmer and cook for 1^1/$_2$ hours. Remove the pan from the heat and leave the veal to cool completely in the stock (this helps keep it moist).

Meanwhile, prepare the tuna mayonnaise. Put the tuna into a food processor along with the lemon juice, capers and anchovy fillets. Add the mayonnaise and process until you have a smooth sauce. Taste for seasoning – the sauce will benefit from a grinding or two of black pepper, but is unlikely to need any salt (as anchovies and capers are both salty). Set aside.

When ready to serve, lift the meat out of the cold stock and place it on a board. Snip off any string and slice with a sharp knife as finely as possible. Cut the tomatoes into big, uneven chunks. Dress the rocket with a squeeze of lemon juice and a few drops of olive oil.

Layer the veal slices on a platter with the tomatoes and rocket leaves. Spoon the tuna mayonnaise on top of the veal, scatter over the olives and capers and finally drizzle over the basil oil. Serve at once, with some good bread.

Roast chicken and bread salad with sour cherries and roasted red onions

I love torn bread salads – the trick is to combine the salad while the bread is still warm, so it can absorb and take on all the flavours. Here, a freshly cooked bird with real flavour is essential – last night's roast chicken will not do. You can replace the chicken with finely sliced Parma ham or, for a meat-free version, lace the bread generously with sweet grilled red peppers and black olives.

Serves 4–6

Roast chicken

1 small free-range organic chicken, about 1.4kg

1 lemon, halved

1 small bunch of thyme

2 bay leaves

small bunch of parsley

5 garlic cloves, halved

1 dried red chilli

olive oil, to drizzle

sea salt and freshly ground black pepper

Salad

2 tbsp dried sour cherries (or cranberries or raisins)

1 loaf of 1-day-old chewy peasant-style bread

about 150ml extra virgin olive oil

1/3 cup Roasted Red Onions (toolbox, page 29)

1 tbsp salted capers, rinsed

1 tbsp finely chopped preserved lemon

2 tbsp saba or good quality balsamic vinegar

large handful of rocket

2–3 tbsp Basil Oil (toolbox, page 42)

finely grated zest of 1 lemon

Preheat the oven to 200°C/Gas 6. Rinse the chicken inside and out and remove the little fat deposits just inside of the cavity. Pat dry. Put one lemon half into the cavity along with the thyme, bay leaves, parsley, garlic and crumbled dried chilli. Squeeze the juice from the other lemon half over the chicken skin, then drizzle with olive oil, massaging it into the skin with your fingers. Season generously with salt and pepper.

Place the chicken in a roasting tray and roast for 15 minutes, then lower the oven setting to 180°C/Gas 4 and roast for a further 45 minutes or until cooked through. To test, pierce the thickest part of the thigh with a skewer – the juices should run clear. Leave to rest in a warm place until cool enough to handle. Pour off the fat from the roasting tray, saving the juices.

For the salad, soak the sour cherries (or other dried fruit) in warm water to cover for 10 minutes. Cut the loaf in half lengthways and tear with your hands into pieces, roughly 3–4cm square. Spread out on a baking tray and drizzle with 2 tbsp extra virgin olive oil. Bake in the oven for about 8–10 minutes until golden brown.

Tip the bread into a large salad bowl. While it is still warm, drizzle over extra virgin olive oil, adjusting the quantity as necessary – the bread should not feel dry. Add the roasted red onions, capers, preserved lemon and saba or balsamic vinegar. Toss together with your hands. Drain the cherries and pat dry, then add to the salad.

When the chicken is cool enough to handle, tear the flesh off the bones and cut into bite-sized pieces. Add to the salad and drizzle over the roasting juices. Toss the chicken through, then add the rocket and toss again. Check the seasoning.

Pile the salad into a serving dish, drizzle over the basil oil and sprinkle with lemon zest. Serve straight away, while still just warm.

Rare roast beef salad with green beans, new potatoes and horseradish cream

This tempting salad is a complete meal in itself – perfect for a weekend lunch. The accompanying horseradish cream has a definite kick to it, though you could reduce the grated horseradish for a milder flavour if you prefer.

Serves 4

800g piece best quality fillet of beef

sea salt and freshly ground black pepper

1 tbsp olive oil

600g little new potatoes (ideally Roseval or La Ratte)

300g fine green beans, topped but not tailed

grated zest and juice of ½ lemon

2 tbsp extra virgin olive oil

handful of mixed salad leaves (such as bull's blood and dandelion)

1 tbsp freshly grated Parmesan

8–12 Slow-roasted Tomato halves (toolbox, page 29)

150g Roasted Red Onions (toolbox, page 29)

2 tbsp Basil Oil (toolbox, page 42)

Horseradish cream

200ml crème fraîche

3 tbsp freshly grated horseradish

1 tbsp Dijon mustard

Start by making the horseradish cream. Put the crème fraîche into a bowl and add the freshly grated horseradish and mustard. Stir to combine and season with a pinch of salt to bring out the flavour of the horseradish.

Preheat the oven to 200°C/Gas 6. Trim the meat of any sinew and fat, then season generously all over with salt and pepper. Heat a heavy-based ovenproof frying pan over a high heat, then add the 1 tbsp olive oil. When smoking, add the beef and sear to colour on all sides. Transfer the pan to the oven and roast for 12 minutes. Cover loosely with foil and set aside to rest for 20 minutes.

In the meantime, cook the potatoes in salted water until tender, about 10–15 minutes. Bring another pan of salted water to the boil, add the green beans and blanch for 2 minutes. Drain and refresh in cold water, then pat dry with a clean cloth. Drain the potatoes as soon as they are cooked and cut in half lengthways.

Put the warm potatoes in a bowl, season with a little salt and pepper and dress with the lemon zest, lemon juice and extra virgin olive oil. Allow to cool, then add the salad leaves and green beans. Toss lightly with your hands and sprinkle with the Parmesan.

Slice the beef into 5mm thick slices. Layer the beef slices and salad on serving plates, piling it high and adding 2 or 3 roasted tomato halves, some roasted red onions and a spoonful of horseradish cream to each plate. Finally, drizzle the basil oil over the top and serve!

Broad beans and peas with mint and feta

This is really a little summer side dish. It works well with roasted chicken at room temperature, served with a properly ripe tomato salad and crusty bread on the side. It is also delicious with barbecued butterflied leg of lamb or grilled steaks, but for me, only when the weather is warm. To my mind, it is a dish best eaten outside.

Serves 4

175g freshly podded broad beans

175g freshly podded peas

small bunch of mint (leaves only)

juice of 1/2 lemon

50ml extra virgin olive oil

sea salt and freshly ground black pepper

175g Persian or barrel-oaked feta

1/3 cup Roasted Red Onions (toolbox, page 29)

2 tbsp Basil Oil, or to taste (toolbox, page 42)

finely grated zest of 1/2 lemon, or to taste

Bring a large pan of water to the boil. Add the broad beans, allow the water to come back to the boil and cook for 45 seconds. Remove with a slotted spoon to a colander and refresh under cold water. When cool, slip off the dull greenish grey skins to reveal the limey green beans inside and place these in a bowl.

To blanch the peas, drop them into the same boiling water, return to the boil and cook for 1 minute. Drain and refresh under cold water, then pat dry and add to the broad beans.

Tear the mint and toss through the peas and broad beans. Squeeze over the lemon juice and drizzle with the extra virgin olive oil. Toss to combine and season with a grinding of pepper and perhaps the tiniest amount of salt (if any at all, as the feta will be intensely salty).

Slice the feta into long fine shards, or crumble it between your fingers if you prefer. Pile the salad into serving bowls and surround with the feta. Spoon the roasted onions over the salad. Drizzle with basil oil and sprinkle with lemon zest to serve.

Double podding broad beans may seem a bit tedious, but it transforms them from a tough, dull vegetable into tender beans that are beautiful to look at and a treat to eat.

Sweet potato and goat's cheese frittata

This frittata often appears as a very thin slice on our mezze plate. I love to eat it on its own though, with a simple herby green salad, like the one we serve with the mezze (see page 69). Use the best quality organic, free-range eggs that you can find – their flavour will make all the difference.

Serves 4

1 medium sweet potato (or 2 small ones)

sea salt and freshly ground black pepper

250g fresh, young rindless goat's cheese

1/2 cup Roasted Red Onions (toolbox, page 29)

75ml Basil Oil (toolbox, page 42)

60g Parmesan, freshly grated

10 organic free-range eggs

1 tbsp olive oil

Preheat the oven to 170°C/Gas 3. Peel the sweet potato, cut into chunks and place in a saucepan. Cover with cold water, add a pinch of salt and bring to the boil. Lower the heat and simmer until tender, about 15 minutes. Drain and tip into a large bowl.

While the sweet potato is still warm, crumble the goat's cheese into the bowl. Toss in the roasted red onions, spoon over the basil oil and sprinkle with the Parmesan. Toss together lightly and set aside.

Break the eggs into a separate bowl and season generously with salt and plenty of freshly ground black pepper. Whisk to combine.

Place a 20–23cm ovenproof (preferably non-stick) frying pan over a medium heat and add the olive oil. When the pan is hot, add the sweet potato and goat's cheese mixture, distributing it evenly over the base of the pan. Pour in the beaten egg and, using a fork, tease it in between the sweet potato chunks, making sure it gets into all the nooks and crannies.

Lower the heat and cook gently for 3–4 minutes, then place the pan in the oven and cook for a further 10 minutes until firm on the surface but still slightly soft and runny in the centre. The frittata will continue to firm up as it cools out of the oven.

I prefer the taste of this frittata at room temperature, when the flavours are clearer, but of course you can serve it warm if you prefer. Accompany with a mixed leaf and herb salad.

Spinach with garlic, lemon and chilli

I love all vegetables (with the possible exception of okra), but spinach is the one that I am totally devoted to. To me, it is equally appealing eaten hot and at room temperature, and I often crave a mouthful of its inky goodness. This side dish goes with many things, but I particularly like it with simple grilled white fish and pan-fried veal or chicken.

Serves 4

1kg spinach (preferably young spinach leaves or pousse)

60ml extra virgin olive oil

2 garlic cloves, peeled and sliced

1/2 medium red chilli, deseeded and finely sliced

sea salt and freshly ground black pepper

juice of 1/4 lemon

Wash your spinach really well in a couple of changes of cold water. If using young spinach, there is no need to remove the stems. If using bigger spinach leaves, cut out the slightly tough central stem. Shake the leaves dry.

Cook the spinach in several batches in a large sauté pan with just the water clinging to the leaves after washing until only just wilted, then drain in a colander to remove excess liquid. Wipe the pan dry.

Heat the extra virgin olive oil in the sauté pan and add the garlic and sliced chilli. Tip the spinach into the pan and add a generous pinch of salt. Toss to mix – the spinach will look vibrant and glossy with its coating of olive oil.

Squeeze over the lemon juice and add a grinding or two of pepper. Serve immediately.

Meringues with summer fruits and crème anglaise

This dessert is only really wonderful when your fruit is perfect. Don't be tempted to try and recreate it out of summer with fruit that has been flown halfway around the world. Savour it during the summer months using beautiful, fragrant English summer berries and perfectly ripe nectarines.

Serves 8

Meringues
6 egg whites (at room temperature)
pinch of salt
360g caster sugar
3/4 tsp vanilla extract

Crème anglaise
450ml whole milk
150ml double cream
1 vanilla pod, split lengthways
120g caster sugar
6 organic free-range egg yolks

To assemble
4 nectarines
250g strawberries (preferably English)
125g raspberries
icing sugar, to dust

For the meringues, preheat the oven to 150°C/Gas 2. Line a baking tray with baking parchment. Make the meringue, following the method in the dessert toolbox (page 244). It should be stiff and glossy. Using a large serving spoon, shape 8 generous mounds of meringue on the baking tray, spacing them well apart to allow room for expansion. Place in the oven and immediately turn the setting down to 120°C/Gas 1/2. Cook for 45 minutes. Turn off the heat and leave the meringues to cool completely in the oven before removing.

To make the crème anglaise, put the milk and cream in a heavy-based saucepan with the vanilla pod and place over a medium heat. Bring to a simmer, then immediately remove from the heat, cover and leave to infuse for 20 minutes.

Whisk the sugar and egg yolks together in a bowl for a minute or two until the mixture is slightly paler in colour. Return the cream to a low heat to warm through. When it is just hot, pour on to the yolk mixture, stirring with the whisk as you do so.

Pour the custard back into the pan and place back on the lowest possible heat. Now a little patience is required. Take a wooden spoon and using a figure-of-eight motion, stir continuously until the custard thickens enough to cling to the back of the spoon. This may take as long as 10 minutes. (Don't be tempted to turn up the heat, or the eggs may well scramble.) When you have the correct consistency, remove from the heat, strain the custard through a fine sieve into a cold bowl and set aside to cool to room temperature. Then cover and place in the fridge to chill thoroughly.

When ready to serve, halve the nectarines, prise out the stones and cut the flesh into thin slices. Half the strawberries lengthways and combine with the raspberries and nectarine slices.

Pour a generous pool of chilled custard on to on each serving plate and place a meringue in the centre. Pile the fruit next to the meringue, dust with icing sugar and serve straight away.

Raspberry and apricot bread puddings

I must confess that I love bread and butter pudding. There is something so comforting about the soft, velvety taste of homemade custard laced with specks of vanilla, contrasting with the sugary crunch of the golden bread topping. Here, apricots and raspberries lend a slightly lemony, not too sweet, summery taste that makes the pudding feel a touch less indulgent... than in fact it probably is!

Serves 8
small knob of unsalted butter
8 fresh apricots
70g caster sugar, plus 1½ tbsp
1 tbsp apricot liqueur (or amaretto)
4 organic free-range eggs
1 tsp vanilla extract
300ml double cream
300ml whole milk
8 thin slices of white bread, crusts removed
150g raspberries
icing sugar, to dust
pouring cream, to serve

Preheat the oven to 150°C/Gas 2. Lightly grease 8 little individual pudding bowls with butter. Halve the apricots, remove the stones and chop the flesh into small cubes. Place in a bowl and sprinkle with the 1 ½ tbsp sugar. Drizzle over the liqueur and leave to macerate while you make the custard base.

Put the 70g sugar and eggs in a bowl along with the vanilla extract and whisk together until pale and creamy. Add the cream and milk, stir to combine and pass through a fine sieve into a jug.

Layer the bread slices with the raspberries and macerated apricots in the pudding moulds, trimming the bread to fit as necessary. Pour over the custard and leave to stand for 15 minutes.

Stand the pudding bowls in a large baking dish and pour in enough water to come halfway up the sides of the moulds. Carefully place in the oven and bake for 30 minutes.

Serve the puddings warm or, better still, at room temperature. To unmould, run a knife around the inside of the bowls and turn out the puddings on to plates. Dust with icing sugar just before serving. Pass around a jug of cream.

Almond tart with blackberries

I find the simplicity of this dessert very appealing. It is merely a pastry case filled with the classic French frangipane and fresh fruit. You can make it all year round, adapting the fruit to the seasons – plums and quinces in autumn, apples and pears in winter, apricots when they appear in spring. My favourite way to eat it is in the afternoon, accompanied by an espresso coffee and nothing else!

Serves 8–10

250g Pastry (toolbox, page 242, ½ quantity)

flour, to dust

200g blanched almonds

200g caster sugar

200g unsalted butter

1 tsp vanilla extract

6 organic free-range egg yolks

250g blackberries

crème fraîche, to serve

Roll out the pastry on a lightly floured work surface to a large round, about 3mm thick. Using your rolling pin, carefully lift the pastry and drape it over a 25cm flan tin, about 2.5cm deep, with removable base. Press the pastry into the edges and side of the tin and trim the excess pastry away from the rim, so that your tart case looks neat. Prick the base here and there with a fork. Refrigerate for 20 minutes.

Meanwhile, preheat the oven to 180°C/Gas 4. Line the pastry case with greaseproof paper and baking beans and bake 'blind' for 15 minutes. Remove the beans and paper and return to the oven for 5 minutes or until the pastry base is golden brown. Remove from the oven and allow to cool.

For the almond filling, spread the nuts out on a baking tray and warm in the oven for 3–4 minutes. Allow to cool, then grind very coarsely using a pestle and mortar, or by pulsing in a blender.

Cream the sugar and butter together in a bowl, using an electric whisk until smooth and pale, then add the vanilla extract. Add the egg yolks, one at a time, whisking until just combined, then finally incorporate the coarsely ground almonds.

Pour the almond filling into the pastry case, then stud evenly all over with the blackberries. Bake for 30 minutes or until the filling is golden brown. Set aside to cool.

Serve the tart at room temperature, with crème fraîche.

Strawberry granita

This is my favourite granita of all. It reminds me of my teenage years in Sydney, as I would often make a detour with friends to the Roma café, where strawberry granita was served in a macchiato glass with fresh cream poured over the top. We would eat this mouthwatering summer treat accompanied by an espresso and think we were very grown up. I still love the pure, clean explosion of iced strawberry in my mouth, followed by the short, sharp, thick, slightly bitter taste of coffee.

Serves 6
125g caster sugar
250ml water
375g English strawberries
juice of 1/2 lemon
pouring cream, to serve
(optional)

To make the sugar syrup, put the sugar and water into a saucepan over a medium heat to dissolve the sugar. Bring to the boil, turn down the heat and simmer for a couple of minutes. Remove from the heat and set aside until the sugar syrup has cooled.

Hull the strawberries and purée in a blender or food processor with the lemon juice. Pass through a sieve into a bowl. When the sugar syrup is completely cool, combine with the strawberry purée.

Pour the mixture into a shallow freezerproof container and place in the freezer for about 2 hours until partially frozen.

Remove from the freezer and stir up the mixture with a fork, dragging in the frozen granita from the sides. Don't beat it as you would a sorbet – the texture of a granita is not the same, it is meant to be icy and crunchy. Return to the freezer until set.

To serve, scoop the granita into glasses. If you are feeling really decadent, you could add a drizzle of cream.

Autumn

There is a certain, stirring excitement that comes with the change of every season. As ingredients begin to make their yearly re-appearance, like old friends, the thrill for me is indescribable. It's a chance to revisit favourite recipes or try something new. Autumn doesn't disappoint. There are quinces, wild mushrooms, walnuts, apples, cobnuts, game, oily fish such as mackerel, sprats and anchovies, mussels, pumpkins, black cabbage, puntarelle and all those beautifully coloured chards. Like the other seasons, if you choose to pay attention to it, autumn has an extraordinary beauty all of its own.

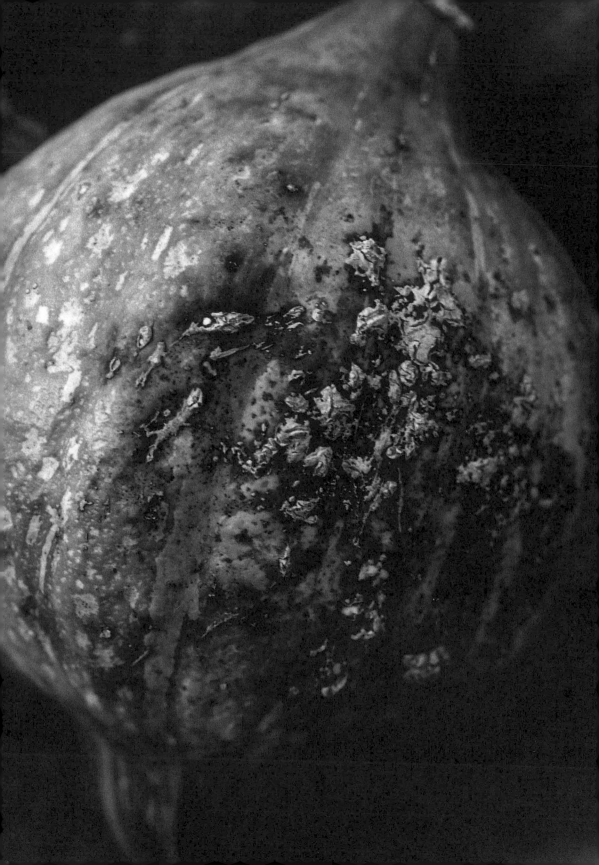

Cauliflower soup with Gorgonzola and pickled pear relish

This is one of my favourite autumn soups. It is a perfect example of agra-dolce, where a sweet, yet sharp relish balances out the deep flavour of the Gorgonzola so it doesn't become overwhelming. For me, it's the perfect lunch, with some textured chewy bread and a simple frisée salad dressed with walnut oil on the side.

Serves 4

1 medium cauliflower

15g unsalted butter

2 smallish yellow onions, peeled and finely sliced

4 thyme sprigs

2 bay leaves

sea salt and freshly ground black pepper

1 litre Chicken Stock (toolbox, page 18)

250g Gorgonzola

100ml crème fraîche

To serve

Pickled Pear Relish (toolbox, page 33)

finely chopped curly parsley

Remove the outer leaves from the cauliflower and break it into small florets (don't bother to remove the stalk – it only adds to the flavour). Melt the butter gently in a saucepan (large enough to hold all your ingredients) over a medium heat. Add the onions and sweat gently for 5 minutes or so until translucent.

Add the cauliflower, thyme and bay leaves. Season with little salt and pepper, to allow the flavours to adjust and find their feet. Pour in the chicken stock, stir and bring to a simmer. Then cover and simmer for 20 minutes or so, until the cauliflower is very soft.

Crumble in the Gorgonzola and stir over a low heat until it has melted into the soup. Add the crème fraîche and stir to combine.

Pick out the bay leaves and thyme stalks, then tip the soup into a blender and whiz until really smooth. This will take a good minute or so, as often one or two little florets escape the blade.

Return the soup to the pan and reheat gently. Taste and add a little more salt and pepper if you think it needs it.

Ladle into warm soup plates and spoon a little pear relish into the centre. Grind a little pepper over the soup, sprinkle with chopped parsley and serve.

Sweet potato and ginger soup

I am very partial to sweet potato. In Australia we eat a lot of pumpkin, squash and sweet potato and these vegetables remind me of home.

Serves 6

2 large sweet potatoes

2 tbsp unsalted butter

2 red onions, peeled and finely sliced

sea salt and freshly ground black pepper

1¹/2 tbsp grated fresh root ginger

1.5 litres Chicken Stock (toolbox, page 18), or water if you prefer

150ml double cream

1 tbsp tamari (or soy sauce), or more to taste

1 tbsp maple syrup

juice of ¹/2 lime, or to taste

Peel and roughly chop the sweet potatoes. Melt the butter in a large saucepan. Add the onions, along with a pinch of salt, and sweat gently for 5 minutes or so until soft and translucent. Now add the ginger, stir, then add the sweet potatoes and stir once more.

Pour in the chicken stock and bring to the boil. Immediately reduce the heat to a simmer and cook gently for 25 minutes or until the sweet potatoes fall apart when prodded with a fork.

Remove from the heat and purée the soup in batches in a blender or food processor (don't fill it more than half full, otherwise the hot liquid might spill out of the top). Strain the soup through a fine sieve back into the pan and reheat gently.

Stir in the cream, tamari and maple syrup, then squeeze in the lime juice. Check for seasoning and flavour – the soup should taste deep, warm, sweet and slightly spicy. If the flavour seems slightly on the surface, just add a little more tamari – it will have a wonderful grounding effect. Serve warm.

Celeriac rémoulade

I first ate this dish in Paris at the age of 19, soon after arriving to further my education. I had been cooking for only a short time and I was at that naive stage of thinking my cooking was about to change the world. I had combinations up my sleeve that no one had seen before…I now realise for good reason. This dish was the first of many lessons I learnt about the beauty, simplicity and elegance of classic French combinations. I often serve it with Parma ham, adding a scattering of toasted Périgord walnuts in autumn, or a tiny drizzle of basil oil in the spring.

Serves 4
1 medium celeriac

Dressing
200ml crème fraîche
1½ tbsp course grain mustard
finely grated zest and juice of ½ lemon
sea salt and freshly ground black pepper

To serve
12 wafer-thin slices of Parma ham
handful of curly parsley, very finely chopped
extra virgin olive oil, to drizzle
handful of walnuts, lightly toasted

First make the dressing. In a bowl, mix the crème fraîche, mustard and lemon zest and juice together. Season well with salt and pepper and set aside while you prepare the celeriac.

Slice off either end of the celeriac, so it sits firmly on a board, then peel away the skin with a sharp knife, following the contours of the vegetable. Then split the celeriac in half lengthways, lay each half flat and slice very finely into half-moon slices. Pile a few of these on top of each other and slice into very fine matchsticks (or julienne). Add to the dressing and repeat to cut up the rest of the slices.

Toss the celeriac julienne in the dressing to coat well and check the seasoning. Spoon on to individual plates and drape the Parma ham slices on top. Sprinkle with chopped parsley, drizzle with a little extra virgin olive oil and scatter over the walnuts to serve.

When I serve dishes cold,
like other chefs, I am referring to food served at room temperature. Anything eaten straight from the fridge doesn't have a chance of displaying any subtlety of flavour.

Wild mushrooms are among autumn's bounty of treasures. Girolles (or chanterelles), ceps, trumpets, honey fungus, porcini and my favourite Kaiser (or uvoli) are all in season. Shaved raw Kaiser mushroom with wafer-thin slices of Parmesan and extra virgin olive oil is something everyone should try... at least once. Newly picked, very fresh mushrooms have an earthy, pungent, meaty flavour when cooked that is rich and deeply satisfying. Each variety has a texture and taste all of its own... it is really up to you to discover your favourites. I prefer to do as little as possible to wild mushrooms. Fussy, complicated recipes only serve to mask their complex and particular flavour. In this case, less is definitely more...

Jerusalem artichokes, porcini and Parmesan hats

This is an adaptation of a dish we prepared at the restaurant for a mushroom event, featuring shavings of rare and expensive Kaiser mushrooms and Parmesan – a classic from the south of Italy. This recipe has a similar feel, celebrates the season in the same way and yet has its very own distinctive quality. I am quite proud of its beauty and simplicity. It only works well as a light first course – it's almost like eating air!

Serves 6

175g Parmesan

200g fresh porcini mushrooms

2 tbsp extra virgin olive oil

finely grated zest and juice of 1 lemon

sea salt and freshly ground black pepper

500g Jerusalem artichokes, scrubbed

1 tbsp very finely chopped curly parsley

about 1 tbsp walnut oil, to drizzle

First make the Parmesan hats – these are incredibly easy. Preheat the oven to 180°C/Gas 4. Line a baking tray with greaseproof paper. Grate the Parmesan on a medium to fine grater and shape into 6 flat circular discs on the baking tray. Place in the oven for 5–6 minutes until melted and lightly golden. Set aside to cool – the hats will firm up as they do so. (They can be kept in an airtight container between sheets of baking parchment for up to a week.)

Gently wipe the porcini with a clean, damp cloth. Using a mandolin, shave the mushrooms lengthways as finely as possible. (If you do not have a mandolin, you should be able to achieve the same effect with a very sharp knife.) Place the porcini shavings in a bowl and toss with 1 tbsp extra virgin olive oil, a third of the lemon zest and a generous squeeze or two of lemon juice. Season with a little salt and pepper and set aside.

Shave the Jerusalem artichokes lengthways very finely. Place in a separate bowl and dress in the same way as the mushrooms, with the remaining olive oil, lemon zest, juice and seasoning.

Layer the Jerusalem artichoke and porcini shavings on individual plates or in shallow bowls, alternating the slices. Put the Parmesan hats on top and sprinkle with the chopped parsley. Drizzle a little walnut oil around each plate and serve immediately.

I don't peel Jerusalem artichokes, because I love the contrast of their milky white centre and nutty brown skin. Just wash them well (or scrub the skins if they are very dirty) and pat dry with a cloth.

Mushrooms always have a much better texture and flavour if you leave them alone during cooking as far as possible – a quick toss or two halfway through is plenty. Too much stirring and they are inclined to stew, resulting in a watery texture.

Girolles with fried egg and sourdough breadcrumbs

I use mushrooms as often as I possibly can from late September through to mid December. I adore their pungent earthy flavour and meaty texture. Quick, hot cooking, with as little adornment as possible works best for me. Here I serve them simply with fried eggs and the contrasting crunch of toasted breadcrumbs. Autumn salad leaves – dressed with a vinaigrette of sherry vinegar and walnut oil – are the perfect complement.

Serves 2

500g fresh girolles (golden chanterelles)

50g unsalted butter

sea salt and freshly ground black pepper

2 organic free-range eggs

2 tbsp virgin olive oil

3 tbsp Sourdough Bread-crumbs (toolbox, page 24)

few fresh thyme or roughly chopped rosemary leaves

1 garlic clove, peeled and finely chopped

squeeze of lemon juice

1 tbsp very finely chopped curly parsley

1 tsp red wine vinegar or sherry vinegar

grated zest of 1 lemon, or to taste

Pick over the girolles with your fingers, removing any bits of grass, then wipe gently with a clean, damp cloth. Place a heavy-based frying pan over a medium heat. Add the butter and heat until melted and foaming, then add the mushrooms and season generously with salt and pepper. Increase the heat a little and leave the mushrooms to cook for 3–4 minutes until tender, tossing them just once or twice during cooking.

Meanwhile, cook the eggs. Place a small non-stick frying pan over a medium heat. Add the olive oil and heat until it just starts to smoke. Crack the eggs into the pan and cook to your preference (I like a firm white with a soft yolk centre). Scatter over the breadcrumbs and thyme or rosemary and allow them to just warm through.

When the mushrooms are ready, add the garlic, a squeeze of lemon juice and half of the chopped parsley. Pile on to two warm plates and slide the eggs and breadcrumbs on top. Add the wine vinegar to the warm mushroom pan, stirring to deglaze, then pour over the eggs. Sprinkle with the lemon zest and remaining parsley and serve at once, while piping hot!

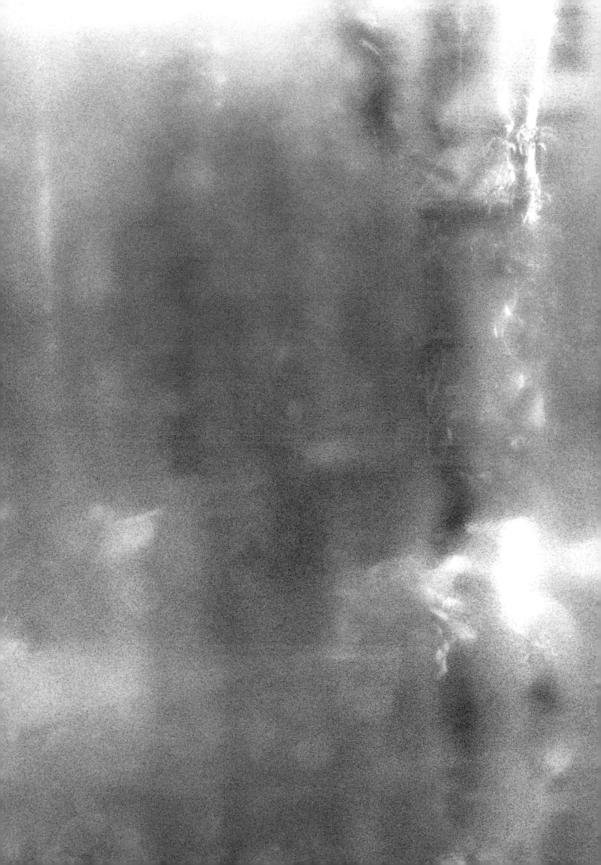

As an accompaniment, this warm salad works really beautifully with roast lamb or grilled white fish, or you can simply serve it on its own with some good bread.

Warm broccoli salad with chilli and garlic oil

The fibrous, leafy, sprouting broccoli that appears in the spring and autumn is one of my favourite vegetables. Cook it correctly in really salted water and its inky green colour is a sight to behold. Here it works brilliantly with the strong, bold flavours of anchovy and chilli. Take the time to infuse your own oil – it will have a flavour far superior to any shop-bought alternative.

Serves 4–6

1kg sprouting broccoli

sea salt and freshly ground black pepper

1 head of treviso or radicchio

good handful of dandelion leaves or frisée

5 good quality canned salted anchovy fillets, chopped

finely grated zest and juice of 1 lemon

1/2 cup Roasted Red Onions (toolbox, page 29)

1 tbsp little black olives (ideally Niçoise or Ligurian)

Chilli and garlic oil

2 garlic cloves, peeled

1 red chilli, halved and deseeded

80ml extra virgin olive oil

Put a large pan of well salted water on to boil (for the broccoli).

In the meantime, prepare the oil. Chop the garlic and chilli as finely as you can. Place both in a bowl, pour on the extra virgin olive oil and leave to infuse while you cook your broccoli.

Tidy up the broccoli by trimming the base of the stalks and removing any leaves that look tired. Plunge into the boiling water and cook for 2 minutes. The stems should still be very crunchy. In the meantime, separate the treviso leaves.

Drain the broccoli, place in a warm bowl and spoon over the infused oil. Add the treviso and dandelion leaves and toss to mix.

Scatter over the anchovies, lemon zest, roasted red onions, a little salt and a grinding of pepper. Lastly squeeze over the lemon juice. Serve at once, piled on to warm plates.

Roasted squash with roasted tomatoes, feta and basil oil

Autumn delivers an amazing array of squashes, pumpkins and gourds. Last year we had the most beautiful display at the nursery, thanks to Geoff Noakes who let us have over 60 varieties. Some were better to cook than others – the onion squash was one of my favourites. If you can't get hold of it, I suggest you use butternut squash instead as its flavour is most reliable.

Serves 4

2 onion squash

3–4 tbsp extra virgin olive oil, to drizzle

1 dried red chilli

small bunch of marjoram, leaves only

sea salt and freshly ground black pepper

500g small plum or cherry tomatoes (on the vine)

175g feta

2–3 tbsp Roasted Red Onions (toolbox, page 29)

2 tbsp Basil Oil (toolbox, page 42)

Preheat the oven to 180°C/Gas 4. Using a sharp knife, cut each squash into 4 wedges and scrape out the seeds with a spoon. Lay the squash wedges, flesh side up, on a baking tray and drizzle with olive oil. Crumble over the dried chilli and scatter over the marjoram leaves. Season with a generous pinch of salt. Roast in the oven for about 35 minutes until the squash is soft and slightly caramelised around the edges.

About halfway through cooking, place the tomatoes on another baking tray. Drizzle with a little olive oil and season with salt and pepper. Roast in the oven, alongside the squash, for 15 minutes. Allow the squash and tomatoes to cool to room temperature. Meanwhile, cut the feta into thin slices.

To assemble, pile the roasted squash wedges and tomatoes on to individual plates or in shallow bowls and scatter over the roasted red onions. Arrange the feta on top and/or next to the squash, then spoon over the basil oil and a little more extra virgin olive oil. Now you are ready to serve!

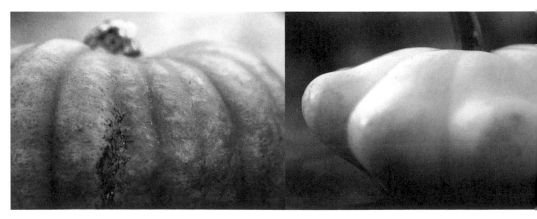

Spiced aubergine and sweet potato with spinach

This is a lovely fragrant curry. The sweet potato and aubergine absorb all the beautiful complex flavours that are laid down at the start of the dish. I particularly like to eat it with a simple flat bread, but it's also good with boiled rice. A cucumber salad with mint and coriander – dressed with lime juice, fish sauce and sesame oil – is an ideal side dish.

Serves 4

500g aubergines, trimmed

sea salt

500g sweet potatoes

2 lemongrass stalks

2 tbsp chopped coriander root and stems

5 garlic cloves, peeled

5cm piece fresh root ginger, peeled

1 large red chilli, stalk removed

6 lime leaves

1–2 tbsp water

4 tbsp vegetable oil

3 red onions, peeled and sliced

1 tbsp Roasted Spice Mix (toolbox, page 16)

1¹/₃ x 400ml cans coconut milk

2 tbsp tamarind water (see page 205)

3 tbsp fish sauce

2 tbsp palm sugar or caster sugar

400g young spinach leaves (pousse), washed

First prepare the aubergines. Cut them in half lengthways and then into 2.5cm cubes. Place in a colander, salt well and set aside to degorge the bitter juices for 10 minutes. Peel the sweet potatoes and cut into 2.5cm cubes.

Meanwhile, peel off the outer layer of the lemongrass, bruise the base with the back off a knife, then cut off and discard the top half (it is dry and unyielding). Put the lemongrass in a food processor along with the coriander root and stems, garlic, ginger, chilli, lime leaves and 1 or 2 tbsp water. Blend for about a minute to a paste.

Pat the aubergine cubes dry with kitchen paper. Place a large, non-stick frying pan over a medium-high heat, add 3 tbsp oil and heat until almost smoking. Fry the aubergine in small batches until golden brown on all sides, then remove and drain on kitchen paper.

Place a large saucepan or cooking pot over a medium heat and add the remaining 1 tbsp oil. When it is hot, add the onions and cook, stirring from time to time, for about 5 minutes until translucent. Add the aromatic paste together with the roasted spice mix and cook, stirring, for 3–4 minutes to release the flavours.

Pour in the coconut milk, then add the tamarind water, fish sauce and sugar. Stir well and bring to the boil, then add the sweet potato. Turn down the heat and simmer for 10 minutes, then add the browned aubergine and cook for a further 5 minutes.

In a separate pan, cook the spinach quickly in batches, with just the water clinging to the leaves from washing, until just wilted. Tip into a sieve and refresh under cold running water, then squeeze dry between the palms of your hands.

Just before serving, add the spinach to the curry and gently warm through. Taste and adjust the seasoning and flavourings if necessary, perhaps adding a little more sugar or fish sauce. You are looking for a balance of sweet, sour, hot and salty flavours.

Mussels with fennel, saffron and spinach

Mussels are at their best during the autumn. I miss them during the summer months when they are not available and begin to pester my fishmonger, Colin, for them early in September. Being a perfectionist, Colin will not sell me anything that is less than perfect…last year he kept me waiting until almost the end of September, but that first batch of mussels was well worth the wait. Plump and deep coral in colour, they are beautiful in this timeless combination. *Illustrated on previous page*

Serves 4

1kg live mussels

1 glass of dry white wine (about 180ml)

2 banana shallots, peeled and finely chopped

4 bay leaves

few thyme sprigs

10 black peppercorns

1 medium fennel bulb

1 tbsp unsalted butter

2 tsp saffron threads

sea salt and freshly ground black pepper

250ml water

250ml crème fraîche

150g young leaf spinach (pousse), well washed

First clean the mussels thoroughly. Remove the tenacious beards, then pull away any seaweed attached to the shell and wash the shells well under cold running water.

Pour the wine into a large heavy-based saucepan, add the shallots, bay leaves, thyme and peppercorns and bring to a simmer. Tip the mussels into the pan, increase the heat slightly and cover with a tight-fitting lid. Cook for 4–5 minutes, shaking the pan now and then to give the mussels room to open.

Meanwhile, prepare the fennel. Trim off the base and discard the fibrous outer layer, then slice finely.

Remove the lid from the pan and tip the mussels into a colander set over a bowl to catch the liquid. Wipe out the saucepan and return to a low heat. Add the butter and once it has melted, put in the fennel slices, saffron and a little salt and pepper (remembering that the mussels may be quite salty). Sweat gently for about 10 minutes until the fennel is soft.

Meanwhile, discard any unopened mussels. Strain the mussel cooking liquor and add it to the fennel with the water and crème fraîche. Stir well and bring to the boil. Simmer for 1–2 minutes, then add the spinach and mussels. Cook for a further minute to wilt the spinach and warm the mussels through. Check the seasoning.

Ladle into warm bowls and serve with crusty open-textured white bread and beautiful unsalted butter.

Griddled scallops with radicchio, sourdough breadcrumbs and anchovy dressing

This salad is full of texture and has a wonderful, intense flavour. The sweet plump scallops work beautifully with it – just make sure you cook them as quickly as possible, so they remain succulent. Allow 4–6 scallops per person, according to size, and ask your fishmonger to shell and clean them for you. You may need to pan-fry the scallops in two batches, depending on the number and your pan.

Serves 4

16–24 scallops (depending on size), shelled and cleaned

2 small heads of radicchio

4 tbsp Sourdough Bread-crumbs (toolbox, page 24)

2 organic free-range eggs, hard-boiled, peeled and grated

1 tbsp finely chopped curly parsley

juice of 1/2 small lemon, or to taste

50ml extra virgin olive oil

olive oil, for cooking

sea salt and freshly ground black pepper

Anchovy vinaigrette

6 fine quality canned anchovy fillets in olive oil, drained

1 shallot, peeled and chopped

11/2 tbsp good quality red wine vinegar

100ml extra virgin olive oil

To finish

finely grated zest of 1 lemon

Set the scallops aside at room temperature while you prepare the salad. Remove any discoloured outer leaves from the radicchio, then cut in half and slice finely (as if you were making a coleslaw). Place in a bowl and add the sourdough breadcrumbs, grated eggs and chopped parsley.

Now make the anchovy vinaigrette. Put the anchovies in a blender with the shallot, wine vinegar and a generous grinding of pepper. With the motor running, slowly pour in the extra virgin olive oil, to create an emulsified sauce. (Don't panic if the sauce splits though, it will still taste delicious.)

Squeeze the lemon juice over the radicchio, drizzle over the extra virgin olive oil and toss lightly with your fingers (easily the best implements for tossing salads). Place a pile of salad on each plate.

Heat a heavy-based frying pan or griddle over a medium heat, then add a good splash of olive oil. Season the scallops well with salt and pepper and, when the pan is smoking, add them to the pan one by one. (Take care as they may well splutter because of their high water content.) Cook for 1 minute, then turn and cook for a minute on the other side. The scallops should have a golden crust on both sides and feel springy when you press them gently.

Lay the scallops on top of the dressed radicchio. Spoon over the anchovy vinaigrette and scatter with lemon zest. Serve immediately, while the scallops are piping hot.

Roasted halibut with Szechuan aubergines

The flavour of these aubergines is based on the style of cooking found in the province of Szechuan in China. Said by some to be the greatest of all Chinese cooking styles, it certainly has a complexity about it that I love. If you can find them, fiery Szechuan peppercorns – roasted and ground – give this dish its final hat. The pickled aubergines would also work brilliantly served cold with slices of rare roast beef or pink lamb.

Serves 4

4 halibut fillets, about 160g each

sea salt and freshly ground black pepper

1¹/2 tbsp olive oil

Pickled aubergines

500g aubergines

bunch of coriander, washed

3 tbsp vegetable oil

5cm piece fresh root ginger, peeled and finely chopped

3 shallots, peeled and finely chopped

4 garlic cloves, peeled and finely chopped

2 tbsp light soy sauce

2 tbsp dark soy sauce

5 tbsp rice wine vinegar

5 tbsp Shaoxing wine (rice wine)

1 tbsp Chilli Oil (toolbox, page 44)

4 tbsp caster sugar

1 tsp Szechuan peppercorns, roasted and ground (optional)

To finish

extra virgin olive oil, to drizzle

First prepare the aubergines. Cut them in half lengthways and then into 2.5cm cubes. Place in a colander, salt well and set aside for 10 minutes. Meanwhile, separate the coriander stems and roots, saving a handful of the leaves. Pound the roots and stems using a pestle and mortar. Pat the aubergine cubes dry with kitchen paper.

Place a wok over a medium-high heat, add the oil and heat until almost smoking. Fry the aubergine cubes in small batches until golden brown on all sides, then remove and drain on kitchen paper.

Pour off excess oil from the wok, then add the ginger, shallots, garlic and pounded coriander root and stems. Stir-fry for a minute or two, then add the soy sauces, rice wine vinegar, Shaoxing wine, chilli oil and finally the sugar. Allow to bubble vigorously for a minute or so.

Return the aubergine to the wok, turn down the heat a little and cook for a further 2 minutes, tossing and turning the aubergine so it absorbs the sweet, sour flavours. Roughly tear the coriander leaves and toss them through the aubergine with the ground Szechuan pepper if using.

To cook the halibut, preheat the oven to 180°C/Gas 4. Season the fish generously with salt and pepper. Heat a large ovenproof pan (that will hold the fish without overcrowding (use two pans if necessary). Add the olive oil and when it is just starting to smoke, lay the halibut, skin side down, in the pan. Cook for 2 minutes without moving or turning, then place the pan in the oven (still without turning the fish) and cook for a further 3 minutes. By now, the skin will be gloriously brown and crunchy.

Place a spoonful or two of the pickled aubergines on each warm plate. Carefully turn the fish and lay it skin side down alongside. Drizzle with extra virgin olive oil and serve.

Pan-fried sea bass with braised fennel and ginger

This is definitely one of my favourite fish dishes...the delicate taste and texture of sea bass work beautifully with the aniseedy flavour of fennel. Beurre blanc complements all white fish – you could substitute halibut, haddock or cod here if you prefer.

Serves 4

4 sea bass fillets (with skin), about 175g each

sea salt and freshly ground black pepper

1–2 tbsp olive oil

1 tbsp very finely chopped parsley (optional)

Braised fennel

6 fennel bulbs

250ml dry white wine

375ml Chicken Stock (toolbox, page 18)

2–3cm piece very fresh root ginger, peeled and cut into matchstick slivers

1 tbsp fennel seeds, roasted and crushed

Beurre blanc

1–2 shallots, peeled and finely chopped

8 black peppercorns

few thyme sprigs

4 tbsp dry white wine, such as Sauvignon Blanc

60ml good quality white wine vinegar

1 tbsp double cream

250g unsalted butter, cut into 2cm cubes and well chilled

sea salt and freshly ground white pepper

Preheat the oven to 180°C/Gas 4. First prepare the fennel. Trim and reserve any feathery fronds for garnish. Remove the fibrous outer layer, cut each bulb into quarters and place in a shallow baking tin. Pour over the white wine and stock, then sprinkle with the ginger and fennel seeds. Cover with foil and bake for 45 minutes until the fennel is soft – it should almost be falling apart.

Meanwhile, make the beurre blanc. Put the shallots, peppercorns, thyme, wine and wine vinegar into a small saucepan. Bring to the boil over a medium heat and reduce until only 1 or 2 tbsp of liquid remain. Strain the liquid, discarding the flavourings and return to the pan. Reduce the heat to very low and add the cream, then gradually begin adding the butter a couple of cubes at a time, whisking continuously to emulsify and taking care that the sauce does not boil. Continue until all the butter is used and you have a creamy, velvety sauce. Season with a little salt and white pepper.

Keep the beurre blanc warm at the back of the stove or in a bowl over a pan of warm water. (It is a delicate sauce and cannot be reheated, otherwise it will curdle). Remove the fennel from the oven when it is cooked and keep warm.

To cook the fish, generously season the skin side only with salt and pepper. Heat the olive oil in a heavy-based ovenproof frying pan (use two pans if necessary to avoid overcrowding). When the oil is very hot, lay the fish gently in the pan and cook without turning until the skin is really crisp; this will take about 4 minutes. Place the pan in the oven for 3–4 minutes to finish cooking.

To serve, spoon a little cooked fennel into the centre of each warm plate. Lay the fish fillets, skin side up, on top and spoon over the beurre blanc. Finish with a scattering of chopped fennel fronds or some very finely chopped parsley.

Pan-roasted guinea fowl with parsley sauce

Parsley sauce reminds me of a warm cotton blanket – cosy and snuggly, but still somehow fresh and clean. The trick is to use a lot of parsley – the sauce should be laden with vibrant green flecks. It goes equally well with poached ham or beef brisket, or you could serve it with poached wild salmon.

Serves 6
6 guinea fowl supremes
sea salt and freshly ground black pepper
a little light olive oil, for cooking

Parsley sauce
150g curly parsley, stems removed, plus extra to serve
500ml double cream
freshly grated nutmeg
1¹/2 tsp finely grated lemon zest, or to taste

First make the parsley sauce. Put a pan of well salted water on to boil (it should be as salty as the sea). Plunge the parsley leaves into the boiling water for 30 seconds. Remove and refresh in iced water (to keep your parsley a beautiful, bright colour). Drain and set aside.

Pour the cream into a heavy-based pan and bring almost to the boil. Turn down the heat and allow to bubble to reduce by about a third, until it has thickened enough to coat the back of a wooden spoon. Add the blanched parsley leaves and boil for a moment longer. Remove from the heat and purée in a blender until you have a beautiful fine texture.

Add a generous grating of nutmeg and the lemon zest, then season well with salt and a good grinding of pepper. Your sauce is now ready; keep it warm.

Guinea fowl has a wonderful depth of flavour and a real warmth that is perfect for autumn. An earthy purée of swede, enriched with butter and seasoned with black pepper, is an excellent accompaniment.

Preheat the oven to 220°C/Gas 7. Season the guinea fowl generously with salt and pepper all over. Place a heavy-based frying pan over a medium-high heat and heat until smoking. Pour in about 1 tbsp olive oil, then brown the guinea fowl in batches. Lay two supremes in the pan, skin side down, and leave to colour for 3 minutes – resist the temptation to play with them. Transfer to a baking tray (without turning) and brown the rest of the supremes in the same way.

Finish cooking the guinea fowl in the oven for 8 minutes or until the skin is crisp and crunchy and the breast meat is succulent, moist and cooked through. Leave to rest in a warm place for 5 minutes.

Arrange the guinea fowl supremes on warm plates, on a bed of swede purée if you like, and ladle the warm parsley sauce generously over the top. Scatter over chopped parsley and serve.

Slow-cooked veal with spinach, carrots and lemon

I haven't particularly come across this dish anywhere before, but it has a sense of classicism about it. As I adore wet food – food you can drag your bread through – I find it very appealing. It works well with a celeriac purée and blanched green beans, tossed with unsalted butter and a little finely chopped garlic. Or you could serve it simply with a baguette and a salad of bitter autumn leaves.

Serves 6–8

2.5kg shoulder of veal

1 tbsp olive oil

sea salt and freshly ground black pepper

3 yellow onions, peeled and sliced

juice of 1 lemon

1¹/2 tbsp Dijon mustard

5 carrots, peeled and cut into big chunks

3 garlic cloves, peeled and finely chopped

few thyme sprigs

3–4 bay leaves

1.5 litres veal or Chicken Stock (toolbox, page 18)

150g young leaf spinach (pousse), well washed

200ml crème fraîche

Trim the veal of any fat and cut into big chunks (about 7cm). Heat the olive oil in a large flameproof casserole over a medium heat. Season the meat all over with salt and pepper. When the oil is really hot, brown the veal a few pieces at a time, turning them to colour evenly. (It is important not to crowd the pan otherwise the meat will stew.) Once the pieces are golden brown all over, remove from the pan and set aside on a plate while you brown the rest in batches.

Lower the heat slightly, add the onions to the casserole and cook for 4–5 minutes until translucent. Squeeze over the lemon juice and stir well to deglaze. Add the mustard, carrots, garlic, thyme and bay leaves. Sauté briefly, then pour in the stock and simmer for a few minutes. Return the meat to the casserole and turn the heat down to very low. Put the lid on, then leave alone to cook for 40–45 minutes.

Meanwhile, place a large saucepan over a medium heat and add the spinach with just the water clinging to the leaves after washing. (This will be sufficient to create steam to wilt the spinach.) Once the leaves have wilted, drain and refresh in cold water, then tip into a colander and drain well. Using your hands, squeeze out as much excess water as possible and set the spinach aside until needed.

After 45 minutes the veal should be tender and the stock will have a rich, warming taste. Discard the herbs, then add the crème fraîche and increase the heat a little – to enable the sauce to slowly reduce and thicken. This will take 10 minutes or so. Taste and adjust the seasoning – you'll probably need a generous grinding of pepper and a good pinch of salt. Finally add the spinach, stir through and serve.

Slow-cooked dishes

work better if the pieces of meat are generous in size. They tend to shrink during cooking and, if you're not careful, you can end up with something resembling a school dinner. Food to me must always be identifiable.

Lamb with sprouting broccoli, anchovy and harissa

This dish is strong, honest and punchy and its colours work beautifully on a plate. Surprisingly, perhaps, anchovies are brilliant with both lamb and broccoli. Harissa is a hot, spicy Moroccan paste, traditionally made with dried chillies. I prefer a gentler version so I make it with fresh chillies and red peppers – the taste is smoother and warmer. You can, of course, add more chillies if you wish. Ask your butcher to butterfly (bone out) the lamb for you.

Serves 6–8

1 leg of lamb, butterflied

5 anchovy fillets in oil, drained and cut in half

2–3 garlic cloves, peeled and cut into slivers

100g unsalted butter, softened

sea salt and freshly ground black pepper

Harissa

2 tbsp Roasted Spice Mix (toolbox, page 16)

2 red peppers, skinned, cored and deseeded

4 garlic cloves, peeled

pinch of sea salt

80ml extra virgin olive oil

5 red chillies, thinly sliced

bunch of coriander, washed and roughly chopped

1 tsp fish sauce

25g palm sugar

few drops of lemon juice

Broccoli

3 generous bunches of sprouting broccoli

1 1/2 tbsp extra virgin olive oil

finely grated zest of 1 lemon

First make the harissa. Put all the ingredients, except the lemon juice, in a blender or food processor and blitz until smooth. Tip into a bowl, stir in a couple of drops of lemon juice and set aside until ready to use.

Preheat the oven to 180°C/Gas 4. Lay the lamb flat, skin side up, on a board and make about 10 small incisions, 1cm deep, all over the surface using a paring knife. Poke 1/2 anchovy fillet and 1 or 2 garlic slivers into each little pocket. Smear the butter all over the skin, using your fingers, then season the lamb liberally with pepper and sparingly with salt. Place in a shallow roasting pan, cover with foil and roast in the oven for 20 minutes.

Remove the foil and return the lamb to the oven for a further 20 minutes to crisp and brown the skin. Because it is butterflied, the meat cooks far more quickly than it would on the bone. It should be pink inside, but not rare. (I much prefer the taste of pink lamb). Cover loosely with foil and set aside in a warm place to rest for 20 minutes. Save the pan juices.

Meanwhile, prepare the broccoli. Trim off the base of the stalks and remove any bruised or damaged leaves. Plunge into a pan of salted boiling water, return to the boil and cook for 2 minutes. Drain and immediately dress with the extra virgin olive oil and lemon zest. Season with a little salt and pepper.

To assemble, carve the lamb into thin slices (or thicker ones if you prefer). Place 2 or 3 slices on each plate and spoon over the pan juices. Lay the broccoli on top of the lamb and spoon over the harissa. Serve at once.

Lamb with prunes, chilli, coriander and spice mix

I really love the process of long slow cooking – how with time, thought and patience, a dish transforms itself from simple ingredients to complex layered flavours that enliven the palate and satisfy the soul. This dish, more than any other, typifies the way I cook. Layering flavours on top of each other, countering the warmth of spices with the cool of lime, balancing salty and sweet flavours. Base notes resonate with top notes to create a harmony that feels just right to me.

Serves 6

1 boned medium leg of lamb

sea salt and freshly ground black pepper

1 tbsp olive oil

generous bunch of coriander

3 red onions, peeled and finely sliced

2–3cm piece very fresh root ginger, peeled and finely chopped

1 tbsp tamarind water (see page 205)

3 garlic cloves, peeled and chopped

2 red chillies, finely chopped (seeds retained)

2 tbsp Roasted Spice Mix (toolbox, page 16)

1.5 litres Chicken Stock (toolbox, page 18)

2 x 400g cans good quality chopped tomatoes

3 or 4 bay leaves

2 cinnamon sticks

100ml tamari, or to taste

75ml maple syrup, or to taste

200g prunes

juice of 1–2 limes, to taste

Cut the lamb into 5cm pieces, trimming away any fat. Season the meat generously with salt and pepper. Place a large heavy-based saucepan over a medium heat and add the olive oil. When it is really hot (starting to smoke), brown the lamb in small batches (to avoid overcrowding the pan). Turn the meat to colour on all sides but don't fiddle with it any more than you need to. As each piece is ready, remove it from the pan and set aside on a plate, while you brown the rest. Wash the coriander, separate the leaves and set aside for garnishing if you like, then finely chop the root and stems.

Once all the meat is browned and put aside, pour off excess fat from the pan, lower the heat slightly and add the onions. Cook, stirring, for 5 minutes or so, until they have begun to soften. Add the ginger, tamarind water, garlic, chillies, spice mix and chopped coriander root and stems. Cook, stirring, for a further 5 minutes. Add the chicken stock, increase the heat a little and bring to the boil. Add the tomatoes, bay leaves and cinnamon and bring back to the boil.

Put the meat back into the pan, cover with the lid and turn the heat down to low. Cook, stirring occasionally, for 45 minutes. After this time, the meat should be almost tender and your base note flavours in place. To balance the flavours, you now need to add the tamari (for salt, depth and colour), maple syrup (for sweetness), prunes (for texture) and lime juice to balance the earthy tones of the spices. Stir well, turn the heat up very slightly and cook for another 30 minutes.

Before serving, check the seasoning and scatter over some roughly torn coriander leaves if you like.

I like to serve this with a sweet potato purée (see page 182) rather than couscous, and a peppery green salad dressed with grated Parmesan, lemon zest, olive oil and lemon juice. A cooling dollop of yoghurt flavoured with a hint of chilli, coriander, lime and olive oil also goes well.

Sweet potato purée with tamari, maple syrup and chilli

This is a punchy, sweet tasting purée, which works particularly well with Middle Eastern flavoured dishes.

Serves 4

2 large sweet potatoes

1 small red chilli, halved (seeds retained)

sea salt and freshly ground black pepper

small bunch of coriander, washed

50g unsalted butter

1 tbsp extra virgin olive oil

2 tbsp tamari (or soy sauce)

2 tbsp maple syrup

Peel the sweet potatoes and cut into rough chunks, then place in a saucepan and add the chilli. Pour in enough cold water to cover, add a good pinch of salt and bring to the boil over a medium heat. Lower the heat and simmer for about 15 minutes until the sweet potato is really tender and falling apart. Drain in a colander.

Tip the sweet potatoes and chilli into a blender. Add the coriander leaves and stems, butter, olive oil, tamari and maple syrup and purée until very smooth. Taste and adjust the seasoning. The purée should have a deep, sweet, hot, velvety taste.

If necessary, return to the pan and reheat gently, stirring, to serve.

As a rule of thumb, all vegetables that grow below the ground go into cold water and all vegetables that grow above ground go into boiling water.

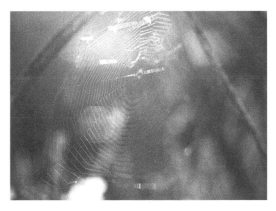

Cavolo nero with garlic and Parmesan

First grown in Italy, this beautiful, ruffled, inky black member of the cabbage family was almost impossible to find outside of Tuscany until a few years ago. Thanks to the work of Ruth Rogers and Rose Gray, it is now available in this country and I love to cook with it. As an accompaniment, this is beautiful with roast lamb, or you can simply serve it as a stand-alone dish – delicious on bruschetta.

Serves 4–6

1kg cavolo nero

sea salt and freshly ground black pepper

100g unsalted butter

1 tbsp extra virgin olive oil

1 red onion, peeled and finely chopped

3 garlic cloves, peeled and finely chopped

150g Parmesan, freshly grated

First wash the cavolo nero in cold water, then drain and cut out the tough white centre, leaving just the crinkly leaves.

Bring a large pan of well salted water to the boil, add the cavolo nero and cook for 2 minutes after the water has returned to the boil. Drain and refresh under cold running water. Drain well.

In a separate pan, melt the butter with the olive oil and add the chopped onion, garlic, a generous pinch of salt and a good grinding of pepper. Sweat gently for about 10 minutes until the onion is soft and translucent.

Add the cabbage and toss well to coat all the leaves in the garlicky butter. When the cavolo nero is warmed through, add the grated Parmesan, toss well and serve.

Autumn coleslaw

This strong, crunchy, earthbound salad comprises everything that is good about autumn – apples, cobnuts, red cabbage and beetroot. My last meal on Earth would have to be some sort of salad…this might just be it! Pretty pink and white candy striped beetroot looks amazing, but the purple or golden variety will taste just as good. If you cannot find cobnuts, use hazelnuts instead.

Serves 4

200g cobnuts, shelled and very roughly chopped

1 pomegranate, quartered

1/4 red cabbage, cored

1 fennel bulb

4 raw beetroot, washed

3 carrots, peeled

4 English apples (preferably Cox's or other Pippins)

small bunch of tarragon, leaves only, finely chopped

sea salt and freshly ground black pepper

1 tbsp extra virgin olive oil

juice of 1/2 lemon, or to taste

Dressing

2 organic free-range egg yolks

1 tbsp honey

1 1/2 tsp Dijon mustard

1 tbsp cream

1 tbsp cider vinegar

1 tsp pomegranate molasses (optional)

200ml mild olive oil

Preheat the oven to 180°C/Gas 4. Spread the cobnuts on a baking tray and gently toast them in the oven for 3–4 minutes, just to release their flavour. Set aside to cool. Carefully extract the seeds from the pomegranate, avoiding the bitter membrane; set aside.

Finely slice the red cabbage into thin ribbons. Cut off the base of the fennel bulb and remove the tough outer layer, then slice very finely. Cut the beetroot into very thin rounds. Shave the carrots into long ribbons, using a swivel vegetable peeler. Quarter and core the apples, leaving the skin on, then slice thinly.

Place the red cabbage, fennel, beetroot, carrots, apples and tarragon in a bowl and season with the salt and pepper. Drizzle over the extra virgin olive oil and squeeze over the lemon juice. Toss gently together with your hands and set aside while you make the dressing.

For the dressing, put the egg yolks into a bowl. Add the honey, mustard, cream, cider vinegar and pomegranate molasses (if using) and whisk together to combine. Season with a little salt and pepper, then pour in the olive oil in a slow stream, whisking as you do so to emulsify. It should have the consistency of a very loose mayonnaise.

Divide the salad among individual plates, piling it high. Drizzle over the dressing and scatter the pomegranate seeds and cobnuts around the plate to serve.

Baked quince with honey, bay and verjuice

Of all the fruits this season offers, I am most excited at the arrival of the first pale green quinces in early autumn. I love the look of our little knarled tree laden with pear-shaped fruit. The way that long, slow cooking transforms quinces into sweet, burnt amber jewels is a constant source of amazement to me.

Serves 4

4 quinces

115ml verjuice

4 tbsp good honey (preferably locally sourced)

2 cinnamon sticks

1 vanilla pod, split in half lengthways

finely pared zest of 1 lemon

4 bay leaves

Greek-style yoghurt, to serve

Preheat the oven to 150°C/Gas 2. Wipe the quinces clean, removing the furry layer with a dry cloth. Quarter them lengthways, but don't bother to remove the pips or core.

Place the quince quarters, cut side up, in a baking tray and pour over the verjuice. Drizzle with the honey and scatter over the cinnamon sticks, vanilla pod, lemon zest and bay leaves.

Cover very lightly with foil and bake for about 2¹/2 hours, turning the fruit halfway through cooking. The quinces are ready when they are soft, sticky and a beautiful burnt orange colour. Serve warm or at room temperature, with Greek-style yoghurt.

Verjuice is made from the juice of unripe grapes. It is slightly tart and adds a little acidity without overpowering the flavours in this dish. If you can't find verjuice, use apple juice instead for this recipe and add a squeeze of lemon juice.

Baked blackberry and stem ginger pudding

I generally prefer clean, light, fresh fruit-based desserts that don't sit heavily at the end of a meal. But as the weather turns cooler and the days become shorter, there is something undeniably comforting about this warm, sweet pudding and the slightly spicy aroma that emerges when you plunge your spoon in. Pair it with a beautiful, thick unpasteurised cream and you have a really lovely autumn dessert.

Serves 4

100g unsalted butter, softened, plus extra to grease

100g caster sugar

2 organic free-range eggs

100g self-raising flour

finely grated zest of 2 lemons

4 knobs of preserved stem ginger in syrup, drained and very finely chopped

a little pinch of salt

4 tbsp golden syrup

12 plump blackberries

thick Jersey cream, to serve

Preheat the oven to 180°C/Gas 4. Butter 4 dariole moulds or small individual pudding basins and set aside. Cream the softened butter and sugar together until pale and smooth. Add the eggs, one at a time, beating well after each addition. Sift in the flour from a good height and fold in gently. Finally, add the lemon zest, stem ginger and a restrained pinch of salt. Fold in until evenly mixed.

Put 1 tbsp golden syrup and 3 blackberries into each pudding mould and spoon the sponge mixture on top. Cover each mould loosely with a piece of buttered foil and stand the moulds on a baking tray. Bake for 30 minutes until well risen and cooked through. To test, stick a skewer into the centre; it should come out clean.

Run a knife around each pudding and turn out on to a warm plate. Serve with a jug of rich, yellowy cream.

Apple and eau-de-vie snow

In early October, we get deliveries of rare breed English apples as the country celebrates National Apple Week. We have a set of very old scales on a rickety old table outside the Cafe and sell them by the kilo. The apples are never around for long, as people find their autumnal beauty hard to resist. I take this opportunity to cook with apples as often as possible and this is one of the desserts I love to make. It's not really snow at all — we stole the name because it is vaguely based on the principle.

Serves 6

250g caster sugar

500ml water

1 vanilla pod, split lengthways

6 apples (preferably Cox's or other Pippins)

pinch of ground cinnamon

8 organic free-range egg whites

pinch of sea salt

2 tbsp apple eau-de-vie

First make the sugar syrup. Put the sugar, water and vanilla pod into a heavy-based saucepan over a low heat and stir a couple of times. Once the sugar has dissolved, turn up the heat a little to bring the liquid to a simmer.

In the meantime, peel, core and chop the apples, quite roughly. Add to the sugar syrup and cook for 5–6 minutes, until tender but still holding their shape. Remove from the heat and leave the apple pieces to cool in the liquid. (This allows the sugary vanilla flavour to infuse them.)

Once cooled, remove the apples with a slotted spoon and put them into a food processor or blender with 2 tbsp of the sugar syrup and a pinch of cinnamon. Whiz to a very pale, smooth purée. Set aside.

Whisk the egg whites in a clean bowl with a pinch of salt to firm peaks. Add to the apple purée and whisk lightly to combine.

Pour the mixture into an ice-cream maker and churn (according to your manufacturer's instructions) until the ice cream has just begun to set. Add the eau-de-vie and continue to churn until you have a soft, feathery, light slush. Scoop into glasses and serve at once.

This 'snow' is cold and pure in feel. As you eat it, the coolness is refreshing, yet the intense flavour of the apple eau-de-vie almost warms you at the same time – like a fire in your chest.

Walnut and honey tart

I think this tart originates from Provence, but I can't be absolutely sure. It is one of my favourites and a lovely way to enjoy fresh walnuts during their short season.

Serves 8–10

250g Pastry (toolbox, page 242, ¹/2 quantity)

flour, to dust

400g shelled walnuts (preferably fresh), halved

1 tbsp walnut oil

250g caster sugar

125ml water

6 tbsp thick honey

4 tbsp crème fraîche, plus extra to serve

Roll out the pastry on a lightly floured work surface to a large round, about 3mm thick. Using your rolling pin, carefully lift the pastry and drape it over a 25cm flan tin, about 2.5cm deep, with removable base. Press the pastry into the edges and side of the tin, using your fingers. Trim excess pastry away from the rim, so that your tart case looks neat and prick the base here and there with a fork. Refrigerate for 20 minutes.

Meanwhile, preheat the oven to 180°C/Gas 4. Place the walnuts on a baking tray, drizzle over the walnut oil and toss gently with your hands to coat them in the oil (being careful not to break them up too much). Toast in the oven for 2–3 minutes only, to intensify their flavour. Set aside while you make the caramel.

Put the sugar and water in a heavy-based saucepan over a medium heat to dissolve the sugar, then increase the heat and allow the sugar syrup to bubble until caramelised to a pale amber colour. Immediately tip in the nuts and stir to coat well. Remove from the heat and add the honey and crème fraîche. Mix well with a wooden spoon and set aside to cool.

Line the pastry case with greaseproof paper and baking beans and bake 'blind' for 15 minutes. Remove the beans and paper and return to the oven for 5 minutes or until the pastry base is golden brown. Remove from the oven and allow to cool.

Spread the walnut filling in the pastry case, piling it high so that it looks generous and beautiful. Serve with crème fraîche.

Winter

With its long hours of darkness and a sky that seems to sit so low that it rests on my shoulders, the English winter can seem very bleak to me. It can also feel a little desolate in terms of fruit and vegetables. Once the abundance of autumn has dwindled, we are left with apples, pears, chards and root vegetables, but little else. Fortunately, Italy brings us wonderful bitter winter leaves. Blood oranges, too, are in season. At their best these have a superb, clean flavour – the perfect finish for a rich winter meal. Winter's true saving grace is the desire it arouses to cook long, slow, comforting dishes. For less money at this time of year, we can produce dishes of real substance with complex, intense flavours that are deeply satisfying.

Parma ham with warm chestnuts, rocket and sage oil

The combination of warm chestnuts and Parma ham makes a delicious simple winter salad. Fresh chestnuts are fiddly to prepare but well worth the effort, but if you can't be bothered, use good quality vacuum-packed chestnuts instead.

Serves 4

12 sage leaves

175ml extra virgin olive oil

finely pared zest of 1 lemon, in wide strips

about 30 chestnuts

handful of rocket leaves

12 slices of Parma ham

Start by lightly bruising the sage leaves with a rolling pin or the back of your knife. Place in a small saucepan with the extra virgin olive oil and lemon zest over the lowest possible heat. Warm through gently for 10 minutes, then remove from the heat and set aside.

To prepare the chestnuts, make a small, shallow incision on the flatter end of each one with a small knife, then immerse them in a pan of simmering water and cook for 12 minutes. One by one, remove from the pan and peel away the skin using your small knife, while the chestnut is still warm. Place in the warm infused oil.

When all the chestnuts are peeled and added to the oil, return the
pan to the lowest possible heat. Warm though gently for 10 minutes
to infuse the chestnuts with the sage and lemon oil. Take off the
heat and set aside for 10 minutes or so, to allow the flavours to
adjust to each other.

Just before serving, toss the rocket leaves through the sage-scented
chestnuts. Divide the warm chestnut and rocket salad among
serving plates. Lay a few slices of Parma ham on top and serve.

Treviso or radicchio leaves are an excellent addition
to this winter salad. If
you have some to hand,
simply add a generous
handful of roughly torn
leaves with the rocket.

Salad of pickled pears, walnuts, dandelion and Gorgonzola

I love to use the young, creamy Gorgonzola cheese, sometimes known as dolcelatte (literally, sweet milk). Its rich, slightly sharp creamy texture works beautifully with walnuts and pears. A perfect warm, wintry salad.

Serves 6

200ml red wine

2 bay leaves

1 small thyme sprig

4 juniper berries

50g caster sugar

2 firm, ripe pears (ideally Comice or Conference)

100g freshly shelled walnuts

bunch of white dandelion leaves

bunch of rocket leaves

200g young Gorgonzola (dolcelatte)

3 tbsp Roasted Red Onions (toolbox, page 29)

1 tbsp finely chopped chervil or curly parsley

Dressing

1 tbsp Dijon mustard

2 tbsp good quality red wine vinegar

sea salt and freshly ground black pepper

100ml walnut oil

100ml olive oil

Pour the red wine into a small saucepan and add the bay leaves, thyme, juniper berries and sugar. Slowly bring to a simmer over a medium heat. Meanwhile, peel, quarter and core the pears, then cut each quarter in half lengthways. Add to the pan and poach for 12 minutes. Remove from the heat and leave the pears to cool in the liquid. Their flavour and beautiful ruby colour will intensify as the poaching liquid cools.

In the meantime, shell the walnuts (I gently tap the outside until they crack with a rolling pin). Wash and pat dry the salad leaves. Slice the Gorgonzola into long, fine shards.

For the dressing, put the mustard, wine vinegar and some salt and pepper in a bowl. Whisk in the walnut oil, followed by the olive oil.

To assemble, dress the salad leaves lightly with 1 tbsp or so of the dressing. Pile into the centre of each serving plate and arrange the cheese, pears and roasted red onions attractively around and on top of the leaves. Scatter over the walnuts, sprinkle with chervil and spoon a little more dressing on to each plate. Serve at once.

Panade of slow-cooked onions with Gruyère

Similar to the aquacottas you come across in Italy, a panade is basically a dish cooked with bread. It is essentially simple food.

Serves 4

50g unsalted butter

4 yellow onions, peeled and very finely sliced

1¹/2 tsp caster sugar

sea salt and freshly ground black pepper

50ml apple brandy

1 bay leaf

4 thyme sprigs

750ml Chicken Stock (toolbox, page 18)

To serve

4 slices of good quality white bread

1 garlic clove, halved

120g Gruyère, grated

handful of curly parsley, stalks removed and very finely chopped (optional)

Melt the butter in a heavy-based saucepan over a low heat. Add the onions, sprinkle with the sugar and add a pinch or two of salt. Sweat gently for 20 minutes until very soft. The onions will deepen in colour as the sugar and butter begin to caramelise and their natural sweetness is teased out.

When the onions are really soft, add the brandy and increase the heat to reduce the liquor, cooking off the alcohol. Add the herbs and pour in the chicken stock. Reduce the heat to medium and cook for another 10 minutes or so, or until the stock has reduced slightly and the flavour is deep and intense. Discard the herbs.

Toast the slices of bread until golden brown on both sides. Rub with the cut garlic clove while still hot and place one slice in each warm soup plate. Ladle over the onion broth and sprinkle with the Gruyère. Finish with a grinding of pepper and a sprinkling of parsley if you like. Serve piping hot.

To appreciate the nature of any dish – its subtleties and complexities – you really need to have cooked it several times. It is only then that will you understand its very heart.

Lentil, red pepper and cumin soup

This simple, honest, filling soup features my favourite pale lentils from Umbria in Italy. You could use Puy lentils if you like, or any other pulses you have to hand – adjusting the liquid and cooking time accordingly. I seem to serve the soup differently every time I make it – sometimes adding a handful of grated Parmesan and a spoonful of sage oil, or stirring a spoonful of tamari into each bowl.

Serves 4

1 red onion, peeled

1 leek, washed and trimmed

2 celery sticks

2 carrots, peeled

2 tbsp olive oil

2 red peppers, halved, cored, deseeded and chopped

3 garlic cloves, peeled and chopped

1 tsp cumin seeds, roasted and ground

2 bay leaves

small bunch of lemon thyme (or regular thyme)

200g Castelluccio or Puy lentils

1 litre Chicken Stock (toolbox, page 18) or water

sea salt and freshly ground black pepper

To serve

good handful of curly parsley leaves, very finely chopped

drizzle of Lemon-infused Oil (toolbox, page 44), optional

Dice the onion, leek, celery and carrots. Heat the olive oil in a large saucepan over a medium-low heat. Add the diced vegetables and sweat gently for 5 minutes, stirring frequently. Add the chopped peppers, garlic, cumin seeds, bay leaves and thyme and continue to sweat for another 5 minutes. By now, the onion, leek and celery should be translucent.

Add the lentils, pour in the stock and bring to a simmer. Reduce the heat and cook, uncovered, for about 20 minutes or until the lentils are tender. Discard the herbs and taste for seasoning – it will most likely need a good pinch of salt and a generous grinding of pepper.

Ladle the soup into warm bowls and scatter over lots of chopped parsley. Finish with a drizzle of lemony oil if you like.

Chick peas with chilli, lime, tamarind and coriander

This chickpea dish is one of my favourite comfort foods and I have been making it on a regular basis ever since I tasted something similar many years ago. If I am honest, when feeling indulgent, I like it best with steamed basmati rice, liberally seasoned with sea salt and a generous dollop of ghee! It would also work well as a side dish with slow-cooked lamb that is meltingly falling apart.

Serves 4–6

25g unsalted butter

1 tbsp olive oil

2 red onions, peeled and finely sliced

generous bunch of coriander

3 garlic cloves, peeled and chopped

1 red chilli, deseeded and finely sliced

2.5cm piece fresh root ginger, peeled and chopped

1 tbsp Roasted Spice Mix (toolbox, page 16)

1 tbsp tamarind water (see below)

4 carrots, peeled and chopped into chunky pieces

2 x 400g cans chopped tomatoes

2 cinnamon sticks

400g cooked or canned chick peas, drained and rinsed

100ml maple syrup

100ml tamari

juice of 2–3 limes, to taste

Melt half of the butter in a medium heavy-based saucepan over a gentle heat and heat until foaming. Pour in the olive oil, stir, then add the onions. Sweat gently for 5 minutes until translucent. Meanwhile, wash the coriander, separate the leaves and set aside; finely chop the root and stems – you need 2 tbsp.

Add the garlic, chilli, ginger, coriander roots and stems, spice mix and tamarind water. Stir for a minute or so, then add the carrots, tomatoes and cinnamon. Stir well to combine all the ingredients. Put the lid on, turn the heat to low and cook, stirring occasionally, for 1 hour. By this stage the tomatoes will have broken down into the sauce, the carrots should be almost tender and the flavours really comfortable with each other.

Add the cooked chick peas, maple syrup and tamari and cook for a further 10 minutes or so. Add the remaining butter and lime juice and stir well to combine.

Now it's time to taste. You are looking for a really deep, smooth, spicy, sour, salty and sweet flavour – one that is totally satisfying. If you haven't achieved this, play around a little, pausing to think what might complete the flavour... perhaps a touch more tamari or maple syrup. Finish by stirring a generous handful of coriander leaves through.

Tamarind lends a distinctive sour taste, helping to balance out the sweet, salty and hot flavours so often found in Asian cooking. I buy the whole pod, keep it in a sealed container in the fridge and break off little pieces as I need them. To use, the pieces are soaked in hot water to cover for 20 minutes. The water takes on the tamarind flavour and it is this that you use once it has been strained. Press the tamarind pulp in your strainer to extract as much flavour as possible.

Smoked haddock chowder

This is a wholesome, calm, comforting winter soup. It's really too much as a first course, but it makes a perfect lunch or late night supper – served simply with a salad and bread.

Serves 4–6

1kg undyed smoked haddock fillet

1 litre whole milk

6 black peppercorns

25g unsalted butter

2 rashers of smoked streaky bacon, derinded and chopped

1 leek, washed, trimmed and diced (include a little of the green part)

3 carrots, peeled and diced

3 celery sticks, diced

3 medium potatoes, peeled and chopped

2 lemon thyme sprigs (or regular thyme)

2 bay leaves

sea salt and freshly ground black pepper

100ml double cream

grated zest of 1 lemon

small handful of curly parsley leaves, very finely chopped

Check the fish for any small pin bones. Pour the milk into a wide saucepan, add the peppercorns and place over a medium heat. Bring to just under a simmer, then add the smoked haddock and remove from the heat. Set aside until the haddock is cooled – the heat of the milk will be enough to gently poach the fish.

Meanwhile, melt the butter in another saucepan over a gentle heat. When it is foaming, add the bacon and cook for 2–3 minutes or until lightly browned. Add the leek, carrots, celery, potatoes, thyme and bay leaves and season with a little salt and pepper. Cook over a low heat for 10 minutes or so, until the vegetables begin to soften.

Drain the haddock, reserving the poaching milk. Once the fish is cool, remove the skin and flake the flesh, keeping it in large chunks. Add to the softened vegetables, then strain the milk into the pan (to remove the peppercorns). Turn the heat up very slightly and cook until the potatoes and carrots are tender. It is important that the milk doesn't boil.

Stir in the cream and warm through, then discard the herbs and check the seasoning. Ladle the chowder into warm soup plates and scatter over the lemon zest and finely chopped parsley to serve.

Pan-fried scallops with horseradish cream and winter leaves

You can use any winter leaves for this salad. I favour white dandelion, ruby chard and mizuna, a little chervil thrown in is also rather good. The simple horseradish cream has a delicate balance that does not overpower the sweet scallops. It is also good with mackerel and, of course, rare beef. If serving with beef, add another spoonful of horseradish and a little more mustard for an extra kick if you like.

Serves 4
24 scallops, cleaned
handful of rocket
handful of white dandelion leaves
handful of mizuna
finely grated zest and juice of 1 lemon
1 tbsp extra virgin olive oil
sea salt and freshly ground black pepper
a little olive oil

Horseradish cream
200ml crème fraîche
1 tbsp freshly grated horseradish root
1½ tsp Dijon mustard

To serve
sprinkling of very finely chopped curly parsley
lemon wedges

First make the horseradish cream (a day in advance if you like). Put the crème fraîche in a bowl and fold in the grated horseradish and mustard. Season with salt to taste. (If making ahead, cover and refrigerate, but return to room temperature before serving.)

Have the scallops ready at room temperature. Wash the salad leaves, dry well and combine in a bowl. Dress with the lemon zest and juice and the extra virgin olive oil, then divide among four plates or arrange on a large platter.

Place two heavy-based (ideally non-stick) frying pans over a high heat and allow them to get very hot. Season the scallops lightly with salt and pepper. Drizzle ½ tbsp olive oil into each pan.

When the oil begins to smoke, add the scallops, arranging them in a single layer. It is important not to overcrowd the pan (if you do, the scallops will stew rather than fry), so cook in two batches if necessary. Cook for 1 minute only, then turn (in the same order that you put them into the pan) and cook for the same amount of time on the other side. The scallops should be crunchy and golden on the surface, with a sweet and delicious taste.

As you remove the scallops from the pan, place them on top of the salad leaves, adding a dollop of horseradish cream. Sprinkle with finely chopped parsley and serve straight away, with a wedge or two of lemon on the side.

Scallop coral has a delicate flavour. I always leave it attached when I'm cleaning scallops, but you can remove it if you prefer not to eat it.

Salt cod with tomato, fennel, saffron and aïoli

The base flavours of this dish are reminiscent of a classic French bouillabaisse. They work brilliantly with salt cod, just as they do with the assortment of fish you encounter in a traditional bouillabaisse. The accompanying garlicky aïoli, once stirred in, helps to create a rich and velvety sauce that has a sublime flavour.

Serves 4

800g salt cod (see below)

1 large or 2 small fennel bulbs

good pinch of saffron threads

5 tbsp olive oil

1 medium yellow onion, peeled and chopped

sea salt and freshly ground black pepper

1 medium leek, washed and sliced (including a little of the green part)

4 garlic cloves, peeled and chopped

4 tbsp dry white wine

2 x 400g cans good quality Italian plum tomatoes

3 bay leaves

few thyme sprigs

finely peeled zest of 1 orange

175ml Chicken Stock (toolbox, page 18) or water

2 tbsp black olives (ideally Niçoise or Ligurian)

To serve

Aïoli (toolbox, page 36)

Trim the fennel and cut into 2cm thick wedges. Scatter the saffron in a medium-large flameproof casserole and place over a low heat. When the casserole is just hot to the touch, add the olive oil and quickly swirl to cover the base. Add the chopped onion, fennel and a generous pinch of sea salt. Stir, then cover and cook gently for about 10 minutes, stirring occasionally, until the onion is soft and translucent. Add the leek and garlic and cook for a few minutes.

Pour in the wine and allow it to bubble and evaporate slightly. Add the tomatoes, bay leaves, thyme sprigs, orange zest and a good sprinkling of pepper. Pour in the stock or water, bring to a simmer, cover and cook over a low heat for 15 minutes, stirring occasionally.

Meanwhile, lightly rinse the salt cod and slice at an angle into 4cm thick pieces. Gently place the salt cod slices in the casserole, nestling them among the other ingredients, and add the olives. Bring to a low simmer and cook for 3 minutes, swirling the pan gently once or twice to allow the flavours to get to know each other. Turn off the heat and allow to stand for a minute or two.

Serve straight away, from the casserole, accompanied by the aïoli, a simple green salad and warm crusty bread to soak up the juices.

To home-cure salt cod, ask your fishmonger for a skinned cod fillet. Rinse it under cold running water and gently pat dry, using a clean cloth. Weigh the fish, then lay it on a stainless steel rack, which fits snugly inside a larger pan. Allowing 1½ tbsp good quality sea salt per 500g of fish, season the fillet evenly on both sides, salting the thicker central section more liberally to ensure there is sufficient for curing. Loosely cover the pan with cling film to keep in the smell as far as possible. Leave to cure in the fridge for 3 days, pouring off any liquid and rinsing the bottom of the pan each day. Cod can be home-cured for a week, but this shorter curing gives a delicately flavoured salt cod that is perfect for this dish. Unlike salt cod that you buy, it doesn't need soaking before use, just a light rinsing to remove excess salt.

Chinese five spice is a mixture of Szechua.

Tea-smoked quail with Chinese five spice and buttered spinach

Tea-smoking is an ideal way to cook small, delicate game birds like quail. I serve them with spinach here, but you could substitute Asian greens, such as pak choi, Chinese broccoli or water spinach, as this dish has a definite Asian feel. As always when I use spinach, I am referring to the young, small, bright green leaf, also known as pousse.

Serves 4

1 quantity Tea-smoking Mixture (toolbox, page 20)

2 tbsp Chinese five spice powder

8 quails

300g young leaf spinach (pousse)

1 tbsp groundnut oil

1 tsp sesame oil

1 red chilli, deseeded and very finely chopped

1cm piece fresh root ginger, peeled and finely chopped

2 garlic cloves, peeled and finely chopped

500ml Chicken Stock (toolbox, page 18)

1 tbsp fish sauce

1 tsp palm sugar or caster sugar

1 tbsp lime juice, or to taste

Prepare the tea-smoking mixture, then mix in the five spice powder and set up the tea-smoking equipment as described in the toolbox.

Tea-smoke the quails according to the toolbox instructions, cooking them for 10 minutes. Turn off the heat and leave the quail to stand in the baking tin with the lid on for a further 8 minutes.

Meanwhile, prepare the spinach. First, rinse it well under cold running water until you are sure it is clean. (Spinach needs to be washed thoroughly as it can be very dirty.)

Place a large wok over a high heat. When it is smoking hot, add the groundnut and sesame oils and swirl to coat the base. Add the quail and toss for 2 minutes. Lower the heat slightly, add the chilli, ginger and garlic and cook for a minute to release their flavours.

Ladle in the stock, turn the heat to high and allow to bubble and reduce slightly. Add the fish sauce and sugar and stir well. Finally throw in the spinach and allow it to just wilt and fall. The sauce will make it appear beautiful and glossy.

Take off the heat and finish with a generous squeeze of lime juice. Taste and add a little more if necessary. The sauce should be sweet, pungent, sour, salty and citrusy – all at the same time! Serve at once.

eppercorns, cloves, fennel seeds, star anise and cinnamon, which you can buy as a mix of whole spices or ready ground. If you take the time to roast and grind your own spices (in equal proportions), your Chinese five spice powder will be infinitely better.

Confit of duck with blood orange and fennel salad

Of all the preserving methods, a good confit maintains the natural flavour of the meat most truly and keeps it succulent. If prepared correctly, the meat is not salty in taste. The best way to eat confit of duck is pan-fried or fast-roasted until crispy. Here, I serve it with a simple, yet beautiful blood orange and fennel salad. It works equally as well with a parsnip purée and a simple jus reduction.

Serves 6
1 small bunch of thyme, leaves only, roughly chopped
4 bay leaves, chopped
10 peppercorns, crushed
8 juniper berries, crushed
45g sea salt
6 duck legs

To confit
1.75kg duck or goose fat (ask your butcher)
1/4 bunch of thyme
4 bay leaves

In a small bowl, mix together the thyme, bay leaves, peppercorns, juniper berries and salt. Scatter half of the mixture over the base of a shallow dish. Lay the duck legs side by side and fat side down in the dish, then scatter the remaining mixture over the top. Cover with cling film and refrigerate for 2 days.

Pour off any liquid that has accumulated in the dish, then return to the fridge for a further 2 days. Remove from the fridge and rinse the duck legs under cold running water, then gently pat dry.

To confit, very gently heat the duck or goose fat in a large heavy-based pan with the thyme and bay leaves. When the fat has melted and become translucent, add the duck legs and bring to a low simmer. Turn down the heat and cook very, very slowly for about 2 1/2 hours. When the skin slips off the shin and the bone is exposed, you know that the duck is ready.

Remove from the heat and leave the duck to cool in the fat. When completely cool, carefully transfer the duck legs to a very clean earthenware pot. Reheat the fat in the pan, then pour it over the duck legs, making sure they are totally submerged. Allow to cool, then store in the fridge until ready to eat.

'Confit' is an ancient preserving technique – usually applied to duck, rabbit or pork. To prepare a confit, the meat is first salted and laid down for a few days, then rinsed, dried and cooked gently in fat. After cooling, it can be stored for several months in the fridge.

Salad
2 blood oranges
1 fennel bulb
bunch of dandelion leaves
bunch of rocket
small bunch of chervil
bunch of bull's blood or ruby chard
1 head of treviso

Dressing
juice of 1 blood orange
1 tsp sherry vinegar
1½ tsp Dijon mustard
sea salt and freshly ground black pepper
100ml walnut oil

When you are ready to eat the confit, carefully remove the duck legs from the fat and set aside to bring to room temperature. Preheat the oven to 240°C/Gas 9.

For the salad, peel the oranges with a sharp knife, removing all the pith as well as the skin. Slice into fine pinwheels and carefully prise out any pips. Slice the base off the fennel bulb and remove the fibrous outer layer, then cut the fennel into very fine slices. Wash the salad leaves, pat dry and combine in a salad bowl.

To make the dressing, whisk the blood orange juice, sherry vinegar and mustard together in a bowl to combine and season with a little salt and pepper. Whisk in the walnut oil to make a vinaigrette. Taste and adjust the seasoning if necessary.

Place the duck legs, skin side down, in a heavy-based ovenproof frying pan (or sturdy roasting pan) with 1–2 tbsp of the fat. Warm them gently over a low heat until the fat melts, then transfer to the hot oven. Roast for 15 minutes or until crisp, turning the duck legs once halfway through cooking.

Meanwhile, dress the salad leaves lightly with the dressing, then add the fennel and orange slices and gently toss through. Drain the duck confit on kitchen paper to absorb any fat. Serve warm, with the blood orange and fennel salad.

Pheasant with beetroot and roasted tomato purée

Pheasant is a delicious bird. It has a delicate gamey taste that works well with clean, light flavours. The sweet, mellow combination of puréed slow-roasted tomatoes and cooked beetroot is a perfect match for pan-roasted pheasant breasts. This vibrant purée is equally good with roasted quail, guinea fowl or chicken. *Illustrated on previous page*

Serves 4
8 pheasant breasts (with skin)
sea salt and freshly ground black pepper
a little olive oil

Beetroot and roast tomato purée
3 large, raw beetroot, washed
4 Slow-roasted Tomato halves (toolbox, page 29)
40g unsalted butter
2 tbsp crème fraîche

To serve
extra virgin olive oil, to drizzle
finely chopped curly parsley

First, make the purée. Put the beetroot in a saucepan, add cold water to cover and season with a little salt. Bring to the boil over a high heat, then turn down the heat and simmer until the beetroot is tender when pierced with a fork – this may take a good 40 minutes. Drain and allow the beetroot to cool slightly, then remove the skin and stalk.

Cut the beetroot into rough cubes and place in a blender, along with the roasted tomatoes, butter, crème fraîche and a generous grinding of black pepper and sea salt. Blend to a really smooth purée – it will be a beautiful colour. Taste and adjust the seasoning if necessary.

Preheat the oven to 200°C/Gas 6. Season the pheasant breasts all over with salt and pepper. Place an ovenproof frying pan over a medium-high heat and add a little olive oil. When the pan is hot (almost smoking), add the pheasant breasts, skin side down, and cook for 3 minutes without moving until the skin is golden brown. Transfer the pan to the oven and cook for a further 3 minutes (still without turning the pheasant).

Remove from the oven and leave the pheasant to rest in a warm place for about 10 minutes. Meanwhile, gently reheat the beetroot and tomato purée in a saucepan over a low heat, stirring to prevent it from sticking or burning.

To serve, divide the warm purée among warm plates and lay the pheasant breasts on top. Drizzle with a little extra virgin olive oil and scatter a little chopped parsley over to serve.

Pan-fried veal chops with almond and rosemary aïoli

I love the simplicity of this dish. Veal chops are merely seasoned, pan-fried to a golden, crunchy crust and served with a punchy rosemary and garlic aïoli and wedges of lemon. Plainly cooked spinach, drizzled with the best extra virgin olive oil, is the perfect complement to this dish. I also like to serve a simple, well-seasoned tomato salad on the side, again lightly dressed with good olive oil.

Serves 6

6 veal chops, about 2cm thick

a little extra virgin olive oil

1 tbsp finely chopped tender rosemary leaves

2 tbsp olive oil

sea salt and freshly ground black pepper

juice of 1 lemon

Rosemary and almond aïoli

120g whole blanched almonds

2 tbsp very finely chopped tender rosemary leaves

2 garlic cloves, peeled and finely crushed

3 organic free-range egg yolks

juice of 1 lemon

2 tsp Dijon mustard

200ml extra virgin olive oil

To serve

lemon wedges

First make the aïoli. Preheat the oven to 180°C/Gas 4. Scatter the almonds on a baking tray and warm them in the oven for 5 minutes (to tease out and enhance their natural flavour).

While still warm, whiz the nuts in a blender or pound using a pestle and mortar until coarsely ground. Now follow the basic mayonnaise recipe in the toolbox (page 36), combining the rosemary, garlic and freshly ground almonds with the egg yolks, lemon juice, mustard and seasoning before drizzling in the olive oil.

Rub the veal chops all over with extra virgin olive oil and chopped rosemary. Set aside for 10 minutes to allow the flavours to infuse.

Heat the 2 tbsp olive oil in a large heavy-based frying pan until it is really hot and you can see a faint haze rising from the pan. Season the chops with a generous pinch of salt and a good grinding of pepper. Add the chops to the pan and fry, without moving, for 6 minutes. Turn the chops and cook for 4 minutes on the other side. Add the lemon juice and scrape up the sediment from the bottom of the pan to deglaze it.

Serve the veal chops with the pan juices spooned over, accompanied by the aïoli and lemon wedges.

When pan-frying meat, the trick is to season the meat generously with salt and pepper and to cook it, undisturbed, in a really hot pan. Don't be tempted to prod and turn it every 2 seconds. Leave it alone to develop a deep-coloured, slightly salty, crunchy crust on the outside and the meat will be meltingly tender in the centre. A good squeeze of lemon juice is the perfect counterbalance to a salty crust.

Braised oxtail with ginger, five spice and garlic

I love slow-cooking cheaper cuts of meat and oxtail has a fantastic ability to absorb the wonderful aromatic flavours in this recipe. The result is a sticky, fragrant and beautifully rich meat dish that literally melts in your mouth. A sweet potato purée (see page 182) works really well with this dish or, if you want something a little gentler, steamed rice would be perfect.

Serves 3–4

1kg oxtail, cut into large pieces

1 tbsp vegetable oil

3 red onions, peeled and finely sliced

2.5cm piece fresh root ginger, peeled and finely chopped

2 red chillies, deseeded and chopped

3 garlic cloves, peeled and chopped

bunch of coriander, washed

1 tbsp Chinese five spice powder (preferably freshly prepared, see page 215)

2 x 400g cans good quality chopped tomatoes

1 litre Chicken Stock (toolbox, page 18)

50ml fish sauce

50ml tamari (or soy sauce)

75ml palm sugar or 5 tbsp maple syrup

Put the oxtail into a large pan, cover with cold water and bring to the boil. Lower the heat and simmer for 15 minutes, then pour off the water. Rinse the oxtail thoroughly under cold running water and set aside to drain.

Place a large cooking pot or flameproof casserole over a medium heat and add the oil. When it is hot, add the onions, ginger, chillies and garlic. Turn the heat to low and sweat gently for 10 minutes or until the onions become translucent.

Meanwhile, separate the coriander leaves from the stems and set aside for garnishing if you like. Finely chop the root and stems and add these to the pan with the five spice powder. Stir and cook for a couple of minutes to release the beautiful aromatic flavours.

Add the chopped tomatoes and chicken stock and bring to a gentle simmer, then return the oxtail to the pan, ensuring that the pieces are fully submerged. Braise very gently for 1½ hours or until the oxtail is really soft and sticky.

Add the fish sauce, tamari and sugar or maple syrup. Turn up the heat just slightly and continue to cook for another 20 minutes or so. Taste and adjust the seasoning and flavours a little if you need to. Serve piping hot, garnished with coriander leaves if you so wish.

Cook with feeling and intuition. Trust your judgement when you
are balancing the flavours in a dish – you will know what tastes right. And don't
be intimidated by recipes or unfamiliar ingredients. I continue to make
catastrophic mistakes in my cooking, but I enjoy them almost as much as my
successes now, simply because I learn so much from them.

Spicy meatballs with coriander and sour cherries

Meatballs are one of those crowd-pleasing, homely dishes. Warm and nurturing, to me they are real comfort food. I often serve these spicy meatballs with a purée of sweet potato, but they are equally good with steaming soft, buttery polenta... perhaps even better! You will need a generous bunch of coriander – the stems and roots for the meatballs and sauce, some of the leaves for garnishing.

Serves 4–6

Meatballs
400g minced pork
200g minced beef
75g fresh white breadcrumbs
1 tbsp Roasted Spice Mix (toolbox, page 16)
2 tbsp finely chopped coriander stems and roots
1 red chilli, deseeded and finely chopped
2 garlic cloves, peeled and finely chopped
grated zest of 1 lemon
sea salt and freshly ground black pepper
1 tbsp olive oil

To prepare the meatballs, put the pork and beef mince into a large bowl and add the breadcrumbs, spice mix, coriander, chilli, garlic and lemon zest. Mix together really well, using your hands, until evenly blended, seasoning with a good pinch of salt and a grinding of pepper. Form the mixture into small balls, about 4cm in diameter.

Heat the olive oil in a wide, deep sauté pan, then add the meatballs in a single layer (cooking them in batches if necessary to avoid overcrowding the pan). Turn the heat down slightly and fry until the meatballs are nicely browned underneath, then turn and continue to fry until they are well browned on all sides. When the meatballs are evenly coloured, remove and drain on kitchen paper.

To make the sauce, pour off any excess fat from the pan and add the onions. Sweat gently over a low heat for 5 minutes or so until they are translucent, then add the coriander stems and roots, chillies, ginger and spice mix. Stir and cook for a couple of minutes, then add the lime juice, followed by the chopped tomatoes, garlic and a good pinch of salt.

Bring to a simmer, cover and cook over a low heat for 20 minutes, stirring from time to time, until you have a rich, homogenised sauce. Now, add the maple syrup, tamari and sour cherries and turn the heat up for a moment or two – to allow the flavours to get to know each other.

Sauce

2 red onions, peeled and finely sliced

2 tbsp finely chopped coriander stems and roots

2 medium red chillies, finely sliced

4cm piece fresh root ginger, peeled and finely chopped

1 tbsp Roasted Spice Mix (toolbox, page 16)

juice of 1 lime

2 x 400g cans good quality chopped tomatoes

1 garlic clove, peeled and crushed

2 tbsp maple syrup

2 tbsp tamari (or soy sauce)

75g dried sour cherries (or dried cranberries)

To finish

small handful of coriander leaves

Add the meatballs to the sauce, lower the heat and simmer gently for about 20 minutes until they are cooked through. Remove the meatballs with a slotted spoon to a warm serving dish and keep warm while you make any final adjustments to the sauce.

Taste and assess what is needed... perhaps a little more tamari or maple syrup, or a squeeze of lime juice. What you are looking for is a richly flavoured, distinctly Middle-eastern flavour... warm, spicy, a little sweet, salty and sour all at the same time. When you achieve the right balance, pour the sauce over the meatballs and serve, scattered with roughly torn coriander leaves.

Slow-cooked pork belly with cinnamon, cloves, ginger and star anise

This is a deliciously rich and unctuous winter dish. I like to serve it with braised lentils, but it is also very good with lightly cooked Asian greens, such as pak choi.

Serves 6

2kg piece belly of pork (organic, free-range)

2 cinnamon sticks

3 star anise

1 tsp cloves

1 red chilli

3cm piece fresh root ginger, peeled

6 garlic cloves, peeled

2 tbsp chopped coriander roots and stems

100ml tamari (or soy sauce)

75ml maple syrup

sea salt and freshly ground black pepper

1 tbsp vegetable oil

To serve

Braised Lentils (toolbox, page 22)

Put the pork belly into a large cooking pot (or pan) in which it fits quite snugly and add cold water to cover. Bring to the boil, then immediately turn off the heat and remove the pork from the pan. Drain off the water and rinse out the pan.

One-third fill the pan with cold water and place over a medium heat. Add the pork, this time along with the spices, chilli, ginger, garlic and chopped coriander roots and stems. If there isn't enough liquid to cover the meat, add some more water. Bring to the boil, then turn the heat down and simmer very gently for 1¹/2 hours until the meat is cooked and very tender. If you have the rib end, the meat will have shrunk back to expose the tips of the bone. With a pair of tongs, carefully remove the meat from the pan and set aside.

Turn the heat up under the pan to high and add the tamari and maple syrup. (If you don't want the sauce to taste 'hot', remove the ginger and chilli at this point.) Let the liquid bubble until reduced by half – this will take about 20 minutes. As the sauce reduces, the flavours will become very intense, forming a rich, dark sauce.

In the meantime, slice the pork belly into individual servings – one rib should be enough per person. Season the ribs with a little salt and pepper. Place a heavy-based frying pan over a high heat and add the oil. Heat until the pan is starting to smoke, then add the pork ribs and brown well on both sides until crunchy and golden brown on the surface. Strain the reduced liquour.

To serve, lay a rib on each warm plate (or soup plate) and spoon over the reduced sauce and warm braised lentils. Serve at once.

All oils need to be looked after properly. They don't like heat or too much light because they are easily oxidised and spoiled. Keep the bottles sealed – in a cool, dark cupboard, not right next to the stove. This applies to all oils, including flavoured oils, nut oils and, of course, good quality extra virgin olive oil – a valuable commodity.

Sautéed Savoy cabbage with chilli and garlic oils

Savoy cabbage is a lovely, vibrant winter vegetable that works really well with slow-cooked dishes and vegetable purées, as well as simple grilled white fish.

Serves 4

1 medium Savoy cabbage

sea salt and freshly ground black pepper

1 tbsp Chilli Oil (toolbox, page 44)

1 tbsp Garlic Oil (toolbox, page 44)

finely grated zest of 1 lemon

1¹/2 tbsp very finely chopped curly parsley

To finish

1 medium red chilli, finely shredded

or a squeeze of lemon juice to taste, plus 1 tbsp very finely chopped curly parsley

Remove any damaged outer leaves form the cabbage, retaining those that you can as the dark outer leaves are really beautiful when cooked. With a sharp knife, remove the fibrous central core of the outer leaves and then slice the leaves crossways into fine ribbons. Slice the rest of the cabbage in half lengthways and similarly cut into ribbons (there is no need to remove the core as it is quite tender).

Bring a large pan of water to the boil and add a very generous pinch of salt. Plunge the cabbage into the boiling water and allow to just return to the boil. Immediately tip the cabbage into a colander and drain well, then place in a warm bowl.

Drizzle the chilli and garlic oils over the cabbage and add the lemon zest and chopped parsley. Toss to mix, then taste and add a little seasoning if needed. For an extra kick, scatter over some shredded red chilli. Alternatively, add a generous squeeze of lemon juice and sprinkle with chopped parsley and a good grinding of pepper. Serve straight away, while piping hot!

Parsnip purée with thyme, mustard and crème fraîche

Sweet and nutty in flavour, this is a lovely winter purée. It works well with simple grilled meats and with slow-cooked rabbit and chicken dishes.

Serves 4

1kg parsnips

sea salt and freshly ground black pepper

4 thyme sprigs

1 tbsp Dijon mustard

50g unsalted butter

2 tbsp crème fraîche

pinch of freshly grated nutmeg

Peel and roughly chop the parsnips. Place in a saucepan, cover with cold water and add a good pinch of salt and the thyme sprigs. Bring to the boil over a medium heat, then turn down the heat and simmer for 15 minutes until the parsnips are really tender when pierced with a fork. Remove from the heat and drain in a colander. Discard the thyme sprigs.

Tip the hot parsnips into a blender and add the mustard, butter, crème fraîche and nutmeg. Whiz to a smooth purée. Check for seasoning – you'll probably need to add a little salt and a generous grinding of pepper. If the purée needs to be warmed through, return to the pan and stir over a low heat to reheat before serving.

Blood orange and rosemary jelly

A lovely, light, palate-cleansing dessert, this is jelly as it should be... wobbly, cool and not too sweet. Blood oranges are one of my favourite things. These beautiful, blackberry-scented jewels are usually around from December to March, but they are at their best during January and February – just when winter seems almost too barren to bear. You will need about 10 oranges to obtain the amount of juice you need, depending on their size. As the flesh of blood oranges varies in colour and pattern, so will the depth of colour of this jelly.

Serves 4
600ml freshly squeezed blood orange juice
100g caster sugar
3 rosemary sprigs
3$^{1}/_{2}$ sheets of leaf gelatine (or 11g sachet powdered gelatine, see toolbox, page 246)
sunflower (or other neutral-flavoured) oil, to oil

To serve
blood orange slices and a little freshly squeezed juice

Put the orange juice and sugar into a saucepan. Lay the rosemary sprigs on a board and bruise to release their flavour by pressing them firmly with the handle of your knife, then add to the saucepan. Immerse the gelatine sheets in a bowl of cold water and leave to soften for about 5 minutes.

In the meantime, place the saucepan over a gentle heat to dissolve the sugar. As the juice begins to warm through, it will take on the flavour of the rosemary. When the sugar has completely dissolved and the juice comes just to the boil, take off the heat. Remove the gelatine from the cold water and squeeze to remove excess liquid, then add to the hot orange juice and stir to dissolve. Strain through a sieve into a bowl, to remove any pithy bits and the rosemary.

Lightly oil 4 individual pudding bowls and pour in the jelly. Allow to cool completely, then place in the fridge to set – this will only take 1 or 2 hours. I like to serve these jellies on the day they are made, as they continue to set if you leave them in the fridge for longer and can become too firm.

To serve, place a slice of blood orange on each serving plate and squeeze over a little more juice. To unmould each jelly, briefly dip the base of the mould into warm water, then run a little knife around the rim and invert on to the plate. Serve straight away.

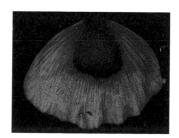

As leaf gelatine varies in potency, you may need to adjust the quantity depending on the brand you are using. My quantity relates to medium-strength gelatine.

Meringues with chestnut purée and cream

When I was 19 and first moved to Paris, a family friend took me to tea at Angelina's, a beautiful and timeless tearoom on the Rue de Rivoli. I ordered a dessert called Mont Blanc – named after the famous snow-capped mountain – and adored it! Even now, it is still my favourite dessert in the world and I serve it at the restaurant in winter. There is something very old-fashioned and elegant in its taste. The nutty, sludgy taste of the chestnut is the perfect foil for the sticky, sweet meringue. A big dollop of buttermilk-coloured unpasteurised cream brings it all together.

Serves 8

Meringue

6 organic free-range egg whites (at room temperature)

pinch of salt

360g caster sugar

3/4 tsp vanilla extract

To serve

small can or jar of sweetened chestnut purée

few drops of lemon juice (optional)

4–6 tbsp thick Jersey cream (preferably unpasteurised)

Preheat the oven to 150°C/Gas 2. Line a baking tray with baking parchment. Make the meringue, following the method in the dessert toolbox (page 244). It should be stiff and glossy. Using a large serving spoon, shape 8 generous mounds of meringue on the baking tray, spacing them well apart to allow room for expansion. Place in the oven and immediately turn the oven setting down to 120°C/Gas 1/2. Cook for 45 minutes. Turn off the heat and leave the meringues to cool completely in the oven before removing.

Place a meringue in the centre of each serving plate. Taste the chestnut purée and add a few drops of lemon juice to counteract the sweetness if necessary. Spoon the cream on top of the meringue and allow it to flow down on to the plate. Place a generous dollop of chestnut purée on top and serve.

The trick is to use a chestnut purée that is not too sweet, so search out a good quality brand that is not overly sweetened. At the restaurant we often make our own purée, but it is labour intensive and not necessary here.

Chocolate 'tart'

This is really a rich, bitter, grown-up chocolate mousse that I bake in a tart tin. It is essential to use a good quality chocolate, such as Valhrona. Blood orange slices are a perfect complement, otherwise a dollop of crème fraîche will suffice. This is a dessert that needs to be served chilled.

Serves 10

butter, to grease

285g good quality dark chocolate (minimum 64% cocoa solids)

565ml double cream

6 organic free-range egg yolks

170g caster sugar

Preheat the oven to 130°C/Gas 1. Butter a 25cm tart tin. Break up the chocolate into small pieces and place in a bowl over a small saucepan of simmering water, making sure the bowl isn't in contact with the water. Allow the chocolate to melt on its own, without stirring. Once melted, remove from the heat and slowly stir in the cream to combine. Allow to cool slightly.

Put the egg yolks and caster sugar in a separate bowl and whisk for 5 minutes until the mixture is pale and doubled in volume. Slowly pour the melted chocolate on to the whisked mixture, stirring gently as you do so.

Place the buttered tart tin on a flat baking tray (to make it easier to negotiate in and out of the oven). Pour in the chocolate mixture and bake for 40 minutes until lightly set – it will still be a little wobbly in the middle.

Carefully remove the tart from the oven and set aside to cool, then chill in the fridge for 1–2 hours. The consistency should be almost like a set mousse. A thin slice is enough for anyone!

Winter rhubarb ice cream

Winter rhubarb is my favourite kind. Its beautiful, pale colour and bitter, limey yellow leaves are lovely to behold. Cooked gently in a little verjuice or water with a spoonful or two of sugar and a vanilla pod, the tender, pink stalks taste wonderful. They also makes a delicious ice cream.

Serves 10

Ice cream base
450ml double cream
150ml whole milk
1 vanilla pod, split lengthways
6 organic free-range egg yolks
120g caster sugar

Rhubarb flavouring
1kg rhubarb
1 vanilla pod, split lengthways
180g caster sugar
250ml verjuice or water

Start by making the custard base for the ice cream, following the method in the dessert toolbox (page 248). Set aside to cool.

Wash and trim the rhubarb, then cut into 5cm chunks. Place in a saucepan with the vanilla pod, sugar and verjuice or water. Place over a medium-low heat and stir gently, just to start the rhubarb off. Bring to a simmer, then turn down the heat and cook very gently for 10 minutes or so, stirring occasionally. The rhubarb should be soft, but not completely falling apart.

Using a slotted spoon, transfer the rhubarb to a bowl. Turn the heat up under the pan and let the liquor bubble until reduced by half. (Rhubarb gives off a lot of liquid during cooking – reducing it down intensifies the flavour.) The reduced liquor should be sharp and sweet at the same time. Pour it over the rhubarb and allow to cool.

Once the custard ice cream base has cooled completely, pour it into your ice-cream maker and churn until thickened. Just before the ice cream sets, pour in the cool rhubarb and churn for a further 10 minutes before serving.

The ice cream will be soft and the colour will be the most beautiful pale, icy winter pink. Spoon into chilled bowls and serve just as it is... to fully appreciate its wonderful flavour.

DESSERT TOOLBOX

The basic recipes and techniques in this section enable you to create many different desserts. Like the main toolbox, the idea of each component is too take one recipe or technique and master it, so you then have the freedom to take it with you through the seasons. I favour simple fruit-based desserts, palate-cleansing sorbets and ice creams, fresh fruit jellies...light as air puddings that don't sit heavily after a main course, but leave you feeling revived and refreshed.

Pastry

This is the recipe I invariably turn to whenever I need a pastry base and it has been a toolbox standby for the past 20 years or so! It is very easy... but then most things are with practice. Technically, it is a pâte sucrée or sweet flan pastry, though I have been known to omit the sugar and add thyme, lemon zest, grated pecorino or Parmesan to use it as the base for a savoury tart.

for the pastry

500g plain flour
pinch of sea salt
250g unsalted butter, chilled and diced into small cubes
50g caster sugar
1 tsp vanilla extract
finely grated zest of 1 lemon
1 organic free-range egg, plus 1 egg yolk
80ml ice-cold water

Sift the flour and salt into a mound on a cool surface. Scatter the butter, sugar, vanilla and lemon zest over the flour, then toss the ingredients together using a knife or pastry scraper. Make a hollow in the middle and add the whole egg, yolk and water and toss again.

Gather the dough close to you and, with the heel of your hand, work it away in a quick movement. Keep bringing the dough back to you and working it until it is evenly combined. (Don't worry if little bits of butter show through, it is important not to overwork the dough.)

Once the dough has come together, continue to knead for a minute or so, very lightly. Wrap the pastry in greaseproof paper and chill for 20 minutes (no longer or it will be too difficult to roll out).

Rolling out and making a tart case

Dust a rolling pin and your surface lightly with flour. Unwrap the pastry, place on the floured surface and start to roll. When the pastry ball has become a flat circular disc, lift and turn it 90°. Dust with flour and continue to roll, turning it from time to time, until the dough is 5mm thick and the desired shape.

Lay the rolling pin on the edge of the pastry and roll the dough around it. Gently lift over the tart case, then unroll the pastry, allowing it to fall loosely over the tin. With your fingertips, lightly press the dough into the sides and base of the tin. With a sharp knife, trim away the extra pastry overhanging the rim. Prick the base all over with a fork and chill the tart case for 25–30 minutes before baking to prevent shrinking during cooking.

To bake the pastry case blind (ie before filling), line the pastry case with greaseproof paper and baking beans and bake, following the guidelines in individual recipes.

Pastry tips

Always use fine quality ingredients – good unsalted butter, very fresh organic free-range eggs and proper vanilla extract, not synthetic vanilla essence.

Work quickly on a cold surface – marble is ideal.

Rest the pastry twice in the fridge (before and after shaping). This helps to prevent shrinking during cooking.

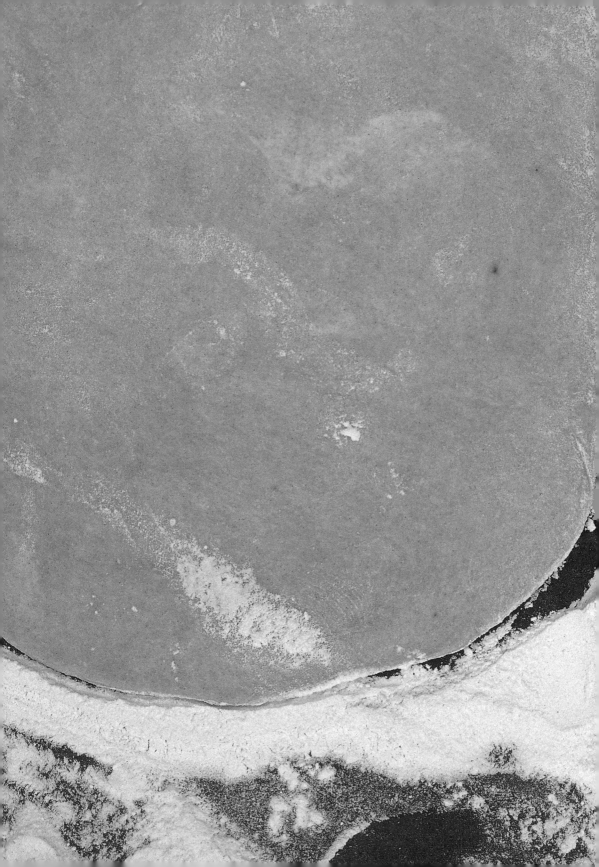

Meringue

I find almost everyone likes meringues. They feel timeless and homely – not like restaurant food at all in my mind. Meringues can, however, be temperamental and need to be treated with respect. They don't like moisture, so they are best cooked in an oven on their own. They also react badly to a sudden change of temperature and are therefore better left to cool completely in the oven, otherwise they are liable to crack. To increase this basic quantity all you have to remember is to allow 60g sugar per egg white.

for the meringue

4 organic free-range egg whites (at room temperature)
pinch of salt
240g caster sugar
1/2 tsp vanilla extract

Preheat the oven to 150°C/Gas 2. Line a baking tray with baking parchment. Put the egg whites in a clean, dry bowl and add the salt (this will help to break down the whites). Using an electric whisk or balloon whisk, beat the egg whites slowly at first until they break down and begin to froth a little. Increase the speed and beat until stiff peaks form (that stay upright without flopping at all). Add the sugar, a spoonful at a time, beating all the while. Finally, beat in the vanilla. The meringue should be stiff and beautifully glossy.

Place generous spoonfuls of meringue on the baking tray, spacing them evenly apart to allow room for them to expand. Place in the oven and immediately turn the oven setting down to 120°C/Gas 1/2. Cook for 45 minutes. Turn off the heat and leave the meringues to cool completely in the oven before removing. Store in an airtight container lined with greaseproof paper for up to 3 days.

Gelatine

l love the pure, palate-cleansing desserts that gelatine enables me to produce. Citrusy fruit jellies and panna cottas, for example, taste wonderfully light and fresh – the perfect finish to a meal. I prefer to work with leaf gelatine as it lends a beautiful texture and is very satisfactory to work with. Delicatessens and some supermarkets stock it, though I concede it is a lot easier to get hold of powdered gelatine in this country. Use whichever you prefer.

Desserts made with gelatine will continue to firm up the longer they stay in the fridge, so don't leave them in too long: 2–3 hours seems to me to be the ideal setting time. When you serve them, panna cottas and jellies should be wibbly wobbly, not overly firm.

Turning out a dessert

To unmould a gelatine-set dessert, briefly dip the base of the mould in hot water, making sure it only comes halfway up the side. Invert a plate on top, then hold the plate and mould firmly together and turn over, to unmould the panna cotta or jelly on to the plate. Serve straight away.

Using leaf gelatine

Leaf gelatines vary significantly in strength, so be guided by the packet instructions, regardless of what your recipe may indicate. As a rough guide, you need to allow about 4 sheets of leaf gelatine per 500–600ml liquid.

Soak gelatine leaves in a bowl of cold water for about 5 minutes to soften before using them. Remove and squeeze out excess water before adding to a mixture.

Always add gelatine to hot (but never boiling) liquid, not the other way round, and stir to ensure it dissolves completely.

Strain the mixture through a fine sieve before pouring into moulds and allow to cool completely before placing in the fridge to set. Keep covered with cling film in the fridge, to ensure that the taste remains pure.

Using powdered gelatine

The same basic guidelines apply. To dissolve, sprinkle powdered gelatine into hot liquid, stirring to dissolve. Powdered gelatine dissolves more easily if it is first softened in cold water and recipes often suggest you do this. Simply put about 4–5 tbsp cold water in a bowl, sprinkle on the gelatine and leave to soften and become spongy for 5 minutes or so.

In general, one 11g sachet sets 500–600ml liquid, but you should follow the packet instructions as not all brands are the same.

Ice cream base

All of my creamy ice creams are based on a simple vanilla custard or crème anglaise, whether they be fruit, chocolate or caramel flavoured. Custard in itself is not difficult to make, but it does require a fair amount of vigilance and care.

The custard needs to be cooked over a very gentle heat and stirred continuously in a figure-of-eight movement, so that it doesn't stick to the bottom. Patience is also required, to obtain the right consistency – you want to achieve a smooth velvety custard.

for the ice cream

450ml double cream
150ml whole milk
1 vanilla pod, split lengthways
6 organic free-range egg yolks
120g caster sugar

Pour the cream and milk into a heavy-based pan and place over a low heat. Scrape the vanilla seeds from the pod and add them to the creamy milk with the empty pod. Slowly bring to just below the boil, remove from the heat and set aside to infuse for 15 minutes.

In the meantime, beat the egg yolks and sugar together in a mixing bowl with a whisk until the mixture becomes thicker and paler. Gently reheat the creamy milk and pour on to the egg yolk mixture, stirring with the whisk as you do so.

Return the custard to the saucepan and place over the lowest possible heat. Stir gently and patiently until the custard thickens – this will take 6–8 minutes (don't be tempted to increase the heat, or you'll have scrambled eggs). It should be thick enough to lightly coat the back of a wooden spoon. Draw a finger along the back of the spoon – it should leave a clear trace.

As soon as the custard thickens, remove from the heat, pour into a bowl and allow to cool. Don't leave it in the saucepan, as the heat of the pan will continue to cook the custard. Once cooled, the custard is ready to use as the base for your ice cream.

Index

The publisher would like to thank Kate
Dyson at the Dining Room shop in
Barnes for the loan of crockery used in
some of the photographs.

Acknowledgements

There are so many people I would like to thank. Firstly, my family, for their enduring love and support, even when I haven't deserved it, including my brilliant sister Briony, my brother David, of whom I am very proud, much-loved members of my extended family – Leila, Eliza, Jeremy, Bella and Ben... and my father, Bruce who I miss dearly. To my mother Ann, who is profoundly talented – her mind is like a magic box full of amazing thoughts and dreams... I love her very much. And, of course, to my two beautiful and extraordinary girls, Holly and Evie, and to James, who I love and whose love and support have been constant.

To Gael and Francesco Boglione, who had a dream to build something beautiful and let me come along for the ride. They are very inspiring to work with, and dear friends.

From the bottom of my heart, I thank everyone I work with at Petersham, including my wonderful kitchen team – Marlon, Dino, Fabio, Suzannah, Ismael, Ros, Clare and others who have come and gone. Also our front-of-house team, notably Jo who has been with us from the start. Special thanks to Rachel Lewis, the best Maître d' I know, and Wendy Fogarty who organises all our events and sources beautiful produce for me to use in the kitchen. Both are more to me than work colleagues... they are treasured friends. I am also grateful to Lucy Boyd who lovingly tends our kitchen garden, and to Sarah Canet, whose guidance has been invaluable. Many have left their mark on Petersham, not least Sophie Cookes, whose year spent in the kitchen with me was an absolute joy!

Thank you to everyone who has worked so hard on this book, including Jane O'Shea at Quadrille who commissioned me in the first place; Janet Illsley, my lovely, patient and gentle editor; Lawrence Morton, for his beautiful design and layout; and to Jason Lowe, whose extraordinary photographs gave me the courage to go ahead with the book. I am especially grateful to the wonderful Lisa Campbell, who has been part of our family for the past six years and who painstakingly typed every single word for this book... thank you, Lisa.

Lastly, I would like to thank all my dedicated producers and suppliers. And the truly inspirational female chefs I admire so much, including Alice Walters, Maggie Beer, Stephanie Alexander, Gay Bilson, Rose Gray and Judy Rodgers, some of whom I have had the privilege to work with. Thank you especially to Layla Sorfie, who was the first to nurture and inspire me!

It was with some trepidation that we purchased the old nursery at the foot of our garden, as we didn't quite know what to do with it. We wanted Petersham Nurseries to be as beautiful as our family home, which we had lovingly restored over five years. So that's how our project began. With the same effort, we set about tossing out the plastic, ripping up the concrete and banishing pesticides... all with the aim of moving to a more sustainable environment. After all, that's the way forward, that's the future.

Day by day the nurseries evolved into a magnificent mish-mash of rambling sweet-smelling jasmine, giant tickling ferns, antique zinc tubs filled with dahlias and rust-spotted urns planted with exquisite miniature roses... all dotted with weird and wonderful pieces from our travels. In such an environment, it was probably inevitable that the nursery would begin to take on an other-worldly feel and a life of its own, both wistful and optimistically modern.

As the nurseries took shape, it became evident that this would be an enticing environment in which to eat some fabulous food. I immediately thought of Skye, who not only cooks as you cannot imagine, but is a person of extreme passion and integrity. Never in my wildest dreams did I think this greatly experienced and talented woman would offer to run a restaurant from a garden shed, but she did! And that's how Petersham Nurseries Cafe was born... from passions shared by like-minded souls.

Petersham Nurseries Cafe is the antithesis of the slick city restaurant. Instead of shiny floors and be-suited waiters, we have dirt on the ground and waitresses in wellies. Yet as inauspicious as it sounds, I think we have taken eating and experiencing food to another level. Skye sources incredible produce and her food is very special. Some describe it as simple, but I have seen her agonise over every last detail. She shares her passion with every mouthful. This book is a testament to Skye and her unique style of cooking... I am so proud of her.

Gael Boglione